FINANCIAL SECURITY
IN THE LAST DAYS

FINANCIAL SECURITY
IN THE LAST DAYS

PERRY STONE

FINANCIAL SECURITY IN THE LAST DAYS
Published by: The International Offices of Voice of Evangelism Ministries
P. O. Box 3595
Cleveland, TN 37320
www.voe.org
423.478.3456

Unless otherwise noted, Scriptures are from the King James Version of the Bible.

Scripture quotations marked AMP are from the Amplified Bible. Old Testament Copyright © 1965, 1987 by the Zondervan Corporation. The Amplified New Testament Copyright © 1954, 1958, 1987 by the Lockman Foundation. Used by permission.

Scripture quotations marked NKJV are from the New King James Version of the Bible. Copyright © 1979, 1980, 1982 by Thomas Nelson, Inc., publishers. Used by permission.

Scripture quotations marked NASB are taken from the NEW AMERICAN STANDARD BIBLE®, Copyright © 1960, 1962, 1963, 1968, 1971, 1972, 1973, 1975, 1977, 1995 by The Lockman Foundation. Used by permission.

Scripture quotations marked NIV are from the Holy Bible, New International Version. Copyright © 1973, 1978, 1984, International Bible Society. Used by permission.

Scripture quotations marked NLT are taken from the Holy Bible, the New Living Translation, Copyright © 1996, 2004, 2007. Used by permission of Tyndale House Publishers, Inc., Carol Stream, Illinois 60188. All rights reserved.

Copyright © 2012 by Perry F. Stone, Jr.
ISBN 978-0-9708611-5-3
First Edition Printing 2012
Cover design by Michael Dutton
Printed in the United States of America

CONTENTS

INTRODUCTION

Early in the year 1999, one of my intercessors named Emie Piper came to see me at our international ministry center. She and her husband Bob would sometimes drop in to chat and hear an update on our most recent conference. But this day was different. Instead of coming to hear a report from the evangelistic field, she came to bring me information she received from the Holy Spirit while praying in the early hours of the morning.

Emie wasted no time telling me, "I was praying much of the night about the economy in America. There is going to be trouble in the future, and it will greatly impact the stock market. The Lord impressed me that in the future, gold will be over $1,000 an ounce, and you and I should invest in it now while the price is low."

I knew two things about Emie. First, she had a strong prayer life; and second, she did receive inspiration and spiritual illumination during her private prayer time. I wanted to share her information with a friend who deals with jewelry, gold, and silver. Within ten minutes we were standing in his jewelry store and Emie was repeating what the Lord had shown her in prayer.

My friend sat at his computer where he could review stocks and commodities. A dedicated Christian, the owner smiled and said, "Today gold is selling at $270 an ounce. I can see it going up to four hundred dollars in the future, and perhaps even five hundred; but not a thousand dollars an ounce."

Emie didn't miss a beat. She understood that, if God is concerned about the sparrow that falls to the ground, He is certainly concerned about the future of His own children, and making sure they discern the times and are properly aligned for God's blessings. She replied, "I know what I felt after praying about God's financial blessings, and you'd better go buy some gold while the price is low. When stocks fall in the future, gold will be high."

As an update, the gold that was selling for $270 an ounce in 1999 is selling, as of this writing, for $1,600 an ounce, for a profit of over thirteen hundred dollars an ounce.

Gold prices will continue to fluctuate in the future. When the global economy improves, gold prices drop. It is possible for gold to fall substantially from its current high prices. In one section of this book, I will talk about gold and silver, and give insight from the ancient Biblical prophecies which reveal certain predictions about precious metals.

With the shaking of the world economies, unsustainable national debt, and high unemployment figures, people are concerned about paying off their mortgages, making car payments, and paying monthly expenses as they provide for their families. Each time gas prices rise, prices of food and other consumer goods increase as a result of higher transportation costs. Each time the journalists speak of more debt, higher inflation, and the possibility of future tax increases, hardworking people wonder if they will make it to the end of the recession.

Many specialists in the field of investments and economics have written books on this topic, and it is not the purpose of this book to repeat what has already been written. My emphasis is to reveal what the prophetic Scriptures teach about money, commodities, and prophetic empires; to teach about financial security from the perspective of God's Covenant; and to show that you must trust God for supernatural provision in every area of your life.

This book will deal with financial security in the last days, but the significant contents of this book are about something more precious than silver and gold. It deals with the instructions for growing spiritually to a new level of faith and understanding how, through various spiritual principles concerning finances and prosperity, a believer can tap into the supernatural provision that has been promised in the New Covenant.

CHAPTER 1

Money and the Rise and Fall of Empires

A MERICA, BY DEFINITION, was not created as an empire but as a republic. We are not ruled by a monarchy or an oligarchy, as empires have been throughout history; instead, we are a sovereign nation ruled by elected representatives who vote on public issues on our behalf. But for decades, America has been a nation of global influence and dominance—sometimes referred to as a super-power. So in that respect, we have some things in common with other nations throughout history that had the governing status and power of an empire.

Empires and superpowers rise through productivity and influence. But eventually they decline through unsustainable debts, war, and loss of respect among other nations. Having studied the major empires of Biblical prophecy for many years, I have identified four important pat-terns that merged in nations or regions of the world, and thus forged an empire on the anvil of history.

For a nation or group of nations to emerge with the power of an empire, their small unit of tribes or individuals must unite with the intent of creating a nation or a power under one leader or form of gov-ernment. As the nation or individuals continue to unify, they develop commerce, currency, and military. Throughout history, the first phase of their dominance was often through military conquest.

The second element is the ability to control commerce in their region (or globally) through their own fiat currency and banking system. Empires throughout history had the power and influence to control the economy and commerce on a regional or even a global scale. Other nations looked to that empire as the strongest economic power in their hemisphere or the strongest nation on earth at that time.

A third characteristic is respect. Other nations—at least for a time—highly regarded the empire and the decisions that were made by the governing authorities. The decisions and actions of a strong nation cause an immediate response by other nations, and the empire's decisions can impact the decisions of the rest of the world. The empire had regional and even global respect and influence. This kind of respect restrains other nations that might be tempted to strategize a military attack against the leading nation.

A fourth trait of such a nation is that their military will be the strongest in the hemisphere, and perhaps even the entire globe. Through their power, they can dominate surrounding nations in the event of a war, and defend their own nation from invaders without and enemies within. They might initiate a major war or bring peace in time of war through their respect, military might, and economic domination.

Before we examine ancient empires, let's look at the nation of America. This country matured from a young cub that was birthed out of the British Empire, to a roaring lion of global authority. What began as thirteen colonies merged into the union of states, called the United States. With leaders who wanted freedom from monarchy, we were created as a republic, a sovereign nation based on liberty and inalienable rights, where power rested with the people who elected their representative leaders.

America enlarged her borders from the original thirteen states to fifty when Hawaii was added in 1959. Since the breakup of the Soviet Union in December of 1991, America has been recognized as the leading military nation. We have been a nation against whose currency the world's purchases and commodity prices have been set. In the past, when our leaders spoke and traveled, they received the highest respect from other world leaders and from people in Europe and other continents. I believe America has been the strongest nation on earth up to this point.

Unfortunately, America is falling into the same trap as empires throughout history that collapsed economically and whose land was overtaken. Those empires of past history began to accumulate high debt and experience internal fighting, like a slow cancer spreading through vital organs. National debt became unsustainable, people were over-taxed to pay for the debt, and they were unable to pay back money they had borrowed at high interest rates.

SIX BIBLICAL EMPIRES

From a Biblical observation, there have been six empires, beginning with the Egyptian empire in the book of Genesis and ending with the Roman empire that existed at the time of Christ's ministry and beyond, into the fifth century.

The Egyptian empire is seen in the latter part of the book of Genesis and the first twelve chapters of Exodus. The second empire was the Assyrian, under whose power the ten northern tribes of Israel were captured and scattered (1 Kings 11:31-35). Eventually the Assyrian monarchy began to decline and was swallowed up by the third empire rising from the ancient land of Shinar.

This empire, ruled by king Nebuchadnezzar, is noted in Scripture as the king and the army of Babylonians that invaded Judea, destroyed Jerusalem, burned the Temple to the ground, and seized the sacred golden vessels from the Temple (Jeremiah 51-52). King Nebuchadnezzar is the central character in the first four chapters of the book of Daniel.

The mighty and wealthy Babylonian empire was eventually over-thrown by the Medes and Persians, who set up their world headquarters in the city of Babylon for 220 years.

The next Biblical empire, the Grecian empire under Alexander the Great, brought an end to the Persian power and a rise in Hellenism, a term identifying the cultural and social influence of the Greeks upon the nations and lands they conquered. The Greek language became the common language in every nation where the Greeks ruled or influenced the government. Even the New Testament was written in the Koine Greek language of the common people.

Finally, the Greek empire capitulated to the Roman empire, which ruled in the time of Christ, the apostles, the early church, and the Apostolic and Anti-Nicene fathers through the fourth century AD. The Western branch of the Roman empire eventually collapsed and was overrun by ten Germanic tribes when the last Roman emperor was disposed in AD 476.

Why did each empire last for only a season and then fall? The simplistic explanation is that each empire engaged in a war with another rising empire and was defeated. A further explanation is that each empire gained economic strength for an extended season, and used their prosperity to construct temples, build cities, and amass a large army. Then eventually, they spent themselves into debt they could not repay.

As their debt and financial obligations to debtors grew larger, the economies of each empire were devastated. Their armies were spread too thin, leaving a rising nation with a stronger economy and military to replace the debt-straddled empire that had become lazy, careless, and left without the resources and skills to defend themselves from invaders and stronger kings.

Historical researchers have pointed out that Babylon was an empire that had hoarded much gold. In their early days, they provided financial loans to the Persians at an interest rate of $33^{1/3}$ percent, to be returned to the Babylonian coffers in the form of gold. The Persians were eventually required to repay double in three years. Thus, the Persians owed a huge and unpayable debt to the Babylonians. Persian commerce eventually slowed to a halt as their creditors went unpaid.

This was one motivation for Cyrus to secretly invade Babylon (see Daniel chapter 5), conquering the mighty Babylonian Empire in 536 BC. The Babylonian leaders were having an all night drunken party when the secret assault was initiated by the Persian king. By invading Babylon, the Persians took control of the temples and treasure houses of the Babylonians. Thus the Persians were able to cancel their massive debt owed to the Babylonians through a war, making Babylon their new headquarters.

The Persians were unaware that the same pattern would be repeated against them and would one day cause their own defeat. The newly-found wealth from the Babylonian coffers enabled the Persians to build cities and strengthen their empire that was controlling 127 provinces (Esther 1:1).

By incorporating the wealth of Babylon and using silver as their currency exchange, the wealth and influence of the Persians spread throughout the known world of that day. Historians say that the Persian soldiers even placed silver embroidered harness on their horses. The Persian government also heavily taxed their provinces. They sent merchants to Greece, and the Greeks began borrowing from the wealthy Persians in order to expand, including loans for the Greeks to expand their navy.

In 421 BC, Sparta—a city in Greece situated on the banks of the River Eurotas—borrowed five thousand talents from the Persian treasuries to build warships. This financial loan, like all others, was at standard $33^{1/3}$ percent interest rates. Seven years later, in 405 BC, Lysander of Sparta used these ships to destroy the whole Athenian fleet which was attacked while they were drawn up on a beach.

This event made Sparta unmatched throughout Greece. These five thousand talents, over a seven-year time frame at $33^{1/3}$ percent, would equal millions of dollars in today's value. Thus, Greece owed a massive debt they were unable to repay to the Persians.

Eventually, Greece was under the dominion of a highly successful and motivated general named Alexander the Great. Using today's monetary standards, Alexander inspected his treasury and discovered only $120,000 in the account. Greece owed nearly $1.5 million in outstanding loans to the Persians. Eventually, the same war cycle was repeated as Alexander the Great and his army battled the king of Persia and his armies, crushing the Persians and taking over the region of Babylon, setting up his headquarters there.

At that time, the Persian government, headquartered in Babylon, had $440 million dollars in gold in their treasury. The result of

Alexander's war with the Persians not only caused a major transition in the ruling empire of that day, it also allowed the Greeks to cancel their loans and inherit huge amounts of land and spoils in a brief time.

The Greeks immediately began to expand and build cities in each land they conquered. In each major city were large temples dedicated to the Greek gods and goddesses. The temple also served as the bank where money (in that day, gold and silver coins) could be stored.

As the Greeks expanded, they also constructed cities in the north and south of Italy, in an area with the Roman Federation positioned in the middle. The Greeks initiated commerce with the Romans, including purchases made on credit using a gold standard.

After the death of Alexander the Great, the Grecian Empire was divided among his four generals, and later those four regions were further divided by internal fighting. Over time, the Romans began to form armies and spread their Roman influence throughout the Mediterranean, expanding their strength in more directions and giving them additional political and military dominion over more nations than any previous empire. Rome eventually became the controlling empire by the time of Christ and the Apostles. In New Testament times, the Roman soldiers were occupying the land now known as Israel and the surrounding nations.

Rome's official rule began with their first elected Emperor, Julius Caesar (known as Caesar Augustus), who ruled from 27 BC to AD 14. He was the emperor when Christ was born in Bethlehem (Luke 2:1). The Roman empire had experienced numerous civil wars and, under Julius, his armies were able to unite the region under his control, ruling from Rome, Italy and spreading Rome's influence throughout Europe and parts of the Middle East. Rome ruled for hundreds of years and was noted for building roads and bridges to connect their towns and cities throughout the empire.

REASONS FOR DECLINE

How can such a mighty empire split between west and east (AD 395), eventually decline, and the western half fall into the hands of barbarians? In his book, *The Decay of Ancient Civilization* by A.E.R. Boak, the writer explains what caused the decline and fall of the Roman Empire. One root cause was high debt and taxation:

> *"The decline and fall of the Roman Empire, that is to say, of ancient civilization as a whole, has two aspects: the political, social, and economic, on the one hand, and the intellectual and spiritual on the other…"*
>
> −PAGE 3

> *"The cities, which had created and sustained the higher forms of economic life, gradually decayed, and the majority of them practically disappeared from the face of the earth."*

> *"…by the third century the burden of taxation had become so heavy that it had begun to consume the capitol resources of the tax payer. This was due to the increasing costs of the imperial administration without any corresponding increase in production on the part of the population of the empire…"*
>
> − PAGE 39

> *"…the increases in taxation coincided with a falling off in production and in manpower. The result was bound to be a heavier weight of taxation for the survivors, and their gradual impoverishment, which, in turn, would cause a decrease in the public revenues."*
>
> − PAGE 40

> *"…the attempt to enforce the economic and social reforms and to extract as large a revenue as possible from the civilian population led to increased departmentalization of the bureaucracy and also to an increase in the number of the civil service employees…this increased the cost of government. This in turn made the burden of the taxpayers still heavier and, under the declining economic conditions, led to further impoverishment …"*
>
> − PAGE 44

DEBASEMENT OF CURRENCY

Several decisions that Roman leaders initiated have also been repeated by former U.S. Presidents and their administrations. Because of government inflation, the Romans began to debase their currency. After 300 BC, the Romans had a gold surplus and began minting gold coins for use in their empire, especially throughout France, Spain and Britain. Silver coins were used in the local and regional areas, with the images of the emperors, gods and goddesses minted on one side. Brass and copper were also used throughout the empire for coins of lesser value.

As time passed, debt increased and inflation ensued, meaning the coins were minted in smaller sizes and the amount of silver was reduced and mixed with a copper alloy. The reason given for the reduction in silver is threefold: inadequate state finances, the eventual lack of the precious metals (silver and gold), and inflation.

The same type of debasement occurred in the United States. At one time our fiat currency (which is paper money that derives its value from government regulation and law) was backed by both gold and silver coinage. The Federal Reserve was required to have forty percent gold backing of its Federal Reserve demand notes, keeping them from expanding the money supply beyond what was allowed by the gold reserves held in their vaults.

With the Great Depression, nations temporarily forsook the gold standard. Eventually we came off the gold standard completely, and it was no longer possible to redeem paper currency for the precious metals. After 1972 the silver half dollars were a mix of alloy and silver, and the quarters and dimes that were once 90% silver are now clad with an alloy. With copper prices rising, in 2012 it cost the U.S. Treasury 2.41 cents to create one copper penny. The Treasury lost $60,200,000 just in 2011 from copper prices exceeding the value of the penny. The old bronze penny that once held ninety-five percent copper is now 97.5% zinc and only covered in 2.5% copper.

NATIONAL DEBT

Another monetary parallel of America's economy to ancient Rome was the level of debt incurred. By the time of Emperor Commodus (AD 180 to 192), the money supply in the Roman government coffers was virtually depleted. Many Americans are unaware that, since 2009, our national debt has increased by nearly five trillion dollars and now exceeds one hundred percent of our gross domestic product.

As of this writing, the national debt is nearly sixteen trillion dollars. The U.S. Treasury debt rating was downgraded in 2011, which is a warning that there is an increased risk that those who invested in bonds and U.S. debt will not get their money back. As with the latter Roman Empire, the idea is to increase taxes on the people, which is similar to applying a small band aid to an amputated leg.

JOB CREATION

The third parallel of Rome with America is related to jobs. In the latter part of the Roman Empire, the primary high paying jobs were those created within the Roman government, especially the government around the area of Rome itself. If you were a politician or fortunate enough to be from an aristocratic family, you could fend quite well for yourself. However, many of the common people turned to government doles, which was a term used for the supply of grain to the city of Rome. In the beginning, citizens purchased the grain, but eventually it was given free. Later emperors added free oil, pork, and wine. The Roman dole would be an early form of the public assistance programs we use today.

Some people abuse such systems, but anytime the middle class begins to disappear as we see happening today, people who were once in the middle class begin to seek government assistance. In recent years, the job growth in America has been weak, with the exception of jobs linked to the state and federal governments. Just as in Rome, these government jobs are some of the highest paying and most secure, while outside of the beltway and capitals, the middle class disappears as they suffer from low pay and a lack of full-time work.

HIGHER TAXES

The fourth pattern being repeated deals with taxes. Rome and all of Italy was a land covered with farms and vineyards, with farmers caring for their personal properties. To maintain the income levels for the government workers, the empire's infrastructure, and the Roman soldiers scattered as peacekeepers throughout the nations, it became necessary for the Roman government to raise taxes. One of the best sources of revenue was to tax the land owners.

In many instances, taxes became so high that the commoners began to quit their jobs to live off the government dole. Eventually a law was passed to prevent working Roman citizens from quitting their jobs, as tax money was needed to provide income for the needs of the government.

Consider America in light of history. The cry of both Rome and America was (and is), tax the rich in order to pay for the runaway spending of the government. In 2012, the co-founder of a social networking site that went public gave up his U.S. citizenship and moved to Singapore—which does not tax capital gains—so that he would not owe taxes on any future appreciation of the company. In 2009, five hundred wealthy people gave up their U.S. citizenship; and by the end of 2011, nearly eighteen hundred had given up their citizenship to avoid paying capital gains and other higher taxes.

In Rome, citizens eventually gave up their farms in frustration, moving to new areas to start over again. The "tax the rich" scheme became the final straw that broke Rome's back. The senatorial class of citizens in Rome—that is, the politicians, nobles, and their families—eventually were charged with a high tax burden, which is believed to have led to financial struggles and the inability to recover economically.

Ancient history from Greece and Rome reveals that in early and latter times, economic decisions made by the government leaders caused individuals to lose their incentives to pursue personal profits and create personal success and wealth. These individuals tired of carrying the weight and burden of oppressive taxes and government regulations placed upon them. The stagnation caused inflation, and the inflation led to debt and the weakening of creativity of the productive class as they lost their desire to work and give most of what they earned to the government.

In summary, the fall of Rome caused the middle class to disappear, and by the 2nd century AD, many Roman-controlled cities had spent so much borrowed money that they were facing debt they could not repay. The cost of repairing the infrastructure, paying the armies, and supporting the government employees had become too great, and the income was unavailable to provide for the needs.

The end result was that the people lost their land as the government bought the farms and the political leaders became rich. At times there were also limits on the food supply, so restrictions were placed on food. Toward the end of the western empire of Rome, the foreign tribes invaded and took over Italy.

In America, many have lost their homes and land, they can't afford to meet their monthly financial obligations, and foreign nations and their corporations have been buying America's foreclosed homes, businesses, factories, commercial buildings, and even large portions of valuable land.

THE DEBT OF AN EMPIRE

It is possible to find pages and pages of articles, charts, and statistics from financial experts who all agree that America's economy is on a collision course due to the nation's level of unsustainable debt. The federal government leaders continue to spend in the hopes it will get them reelected, and for those left paying the bill, there is no end in sight. Maybe you have heard the expression, "we are kicking the can down the road" for elected leaders to deal with. Actually, the road has become a dead end and we are drawing closer to a meltdown. Regulations, laws, and higher taxes are adding to the burden of the productive working people and entrepreneurs in America. For some people it has become more profitable to be on the dole than to be a paid employee.

Those who are paying careful attention and are armed with knowledge will understand the problems facing America. By reviewing secular and Biblical history, we also realize that an empire or a superpower does not last forever, but is eventually replaced by the nation or empire that can control the job markets, the military, and the money—including the lending. America was once a lender, but now we are a borrower. We were once producers but now we are consumers of imports. We were leaders, but now we are followers.

Many are concerned, not only about the future, but about their own economic security. The good news for believers who have received the covenant of redemption through Christ is that the Scriptures are filled with amazing, faith-filled stories of God's intervention in the realm of the basic human needs. He will provide water, shelter, food, finances, employment, tax relief, and every human need mankind will experience.

Throughout this book, we will explore several of these promises and predictions to reveal how blessings are not just created by the hands of men, but are a part of God's own covenant with us. These truths of faith must be mixed with practical understanding and Biblical insight in order to unlock the door of wisdom for financial success, favor and blessing.

CHAPTER 2

Gold and Precious Metals in the Time of the End

"For thus says the LORD of hosts: 'Once more (it is a little while) I will shake heaven and earth, the sea and dry land; and I will shake all nations, and they shall come to the Desire of All Nations, and I will fill this temple with glory,' says the LORD of hosts. The silver is Mine, and the gold is Mine,' says the LORD of hosts'

– HAGGAI 2:6-8 (NKJV)

I T IS INTERESTING that when the children of Israel transitioned from slaves in Egypt to sons of the Most High in the wilderness, in their possession was the gold and silver from Egypt (Ps. 105:37). This gold would not have been the modern gold coins or gold bars that are purchased today by investors, but would have been gold and silver jewelry which was owned by the wealthier Egyptians.

These precious commodities were not for personal investments, but were actually collected in an offering after Moses was given the revelation to construct the Tabernacle in the Wilderness. During this offering, some provided gold, silver and brass; some gave linen and goat's skins; and others offered oil, gemstones and spices for the incense (Exod. 25:1-9). Gold was used to cover the Ark, the Golden Altar, and the Table of Showbread, as well as to construct the candlestick called the Menorah. Certain shovels and smaller vessels were made of gold (Exod. 25:11-39).

The silver came from a silver half–shekel collected from among the Hebrews that was used to form the sockets for the tabernacle planks. An annual half-shekel of silver was collected to fund the purchase of communal offerings for the Tabernacle, and optional gifts of silver were used to make silver vessels. Everyone offered something. This provided the materials for the building of the Tabernacle (which literally means a *dwelling place*).

To show the amount of gold needed for this project, gold is mentioned ninety-two times in relation to the Tabernacle. Twenty-nine talents and 730 shekels of gold were used in the Tabernacle, which totals 1.65 tons of gold (Exod. 38:24). One hundred talents and 1,775 shekels of silver were used, which is 4.8 tons (Exod.38:25-28). The brass amounted to seventy talents and 2,400 shekels, which was 3.3 tons (Exod. 38:29).

Gold was used to construct the furniture in the Holy Place and the Holy of Holies. Gold is a picture of divinity. Pure, refined gold has no impurities, never fades, and never corrupts. Silver is a metal that represents redemption. All males who were numbered in Israel were to give a half-shekel (of silver) as a price of atonement (Exod. 30:13-15). Four silver cups are used during the Jewish Passover Seder, the celebration recalling Israel's redemption. The wooden pillars of the Tabernacle were set in silver sockets, giving a picture that the entire Tabernacle was centered toward the forgiveness of sins and the act of redeeming mankind (Exod. 26:19-32).

The third metal was brass, which is mentioned in thirty-two verses in Exodus in relation to the building of the Tabernacle. Brass represents humanity. The altar in the outer court and the laver were both constructed from brass. The brass altar and laver came from the brass mirrors (called looking glasses in the 1611 KJV) of the women of Israel who provided them in the offering given to Moses (Exod. 38:8).

Just as gold, silver, bronze and other metals were significant in the transition of Israel from Egypt to the Promised Land, there is a parallel occurring today in the earth with precious metals.

THE GOLD STANDARD

Throughout the history of paper (fiat) currency, during times of economic crisis, those who could afford precious metals would invest in gold and silver to diversify their portfolio, provided it was legal to own precious metals. When stocks are low, gold and silver can be sold or used for bartering in the event of economic difficulties.

Centuries ago, when gold was the currency of choice, the nation that had the most gold was the wealthiest. This is why nations throughout history sought gold—so they could be wealthier than other nations. Around the mid-1800s, most countries, including America, began to adopt the gold standard due to world trade transactions. This guaranteed that any amount of fiat currency could be redeemed by that nation for its value in gold, which helped world trade because a country's paper currency now had guaranteed value tied to gold.

By World War I, nearly every country was on a gold standard. When the war began, countries needed money to pay for their military, so they suspended the gold standard and printed money, which devalued their currency and caused hyperinflation. When the war ended, most countries returned to some form of a gold standard.

The gold standard was abandoned once again during the Great Depression. With the stock market crash, people began to invest in commodities and currencies. Those with dollars traded them in for gold because, at that time, the dollar currency was redeemable for gold and silver. This was depleting the federal gold reserves, so the government raised interest rates to try to make the dollar more valuable to those who were saving and investing the money. The government was attempting to keep people from exchanging their currency for gold. However, the higher interest rates had a negative effect on the economy and worsened the depression and unemployment, as it made the cost of doing business so much higher. Companies went bankrupt and more people were out of work.

The Great Depression ended around the time World War II began, and most countries again went on a gold standard. Most adopted the Bretton-Woods System, which set all currency exchange values in terms of gold. The United States held most of the gold, so most countries set the value of their currency to the value of the American dollar. This made the dollar the defacto world currency, which led to an increase in the value of the dollar.

At that time, gold was thirty-five dollars an ounce. Because of the way the financial system worked, the value of the dollar could either cause inflation or stagflation in the United States. Anytime the dollar was devalued, people began to exchange their currency for gold.

Finally, by the end of 1973, the gold standard was dropped. Gold and silver became available for purchase in the free market, and gold quickly increased to $120 an ounce. This caused nations to begin to print more currency, which caused both inflation and economic growth.

With no solid commodity to support the printing of U.S. currency, the value of the dollar is no longer based on a fixed asset. It is now based on the trust and confidence that people have in the American government—sometimes referred to as the full faith and credit of the United States government. The dollar is backed by the goods and services in the economy.

The advantage to being on the gold standard is that it forces fiscal discipline and gives the government less power to manage the economy. The drawback to the gold standard is that a fixed money supply that depends on the backing of gold reserves limits economic growth. Businesses suffer from a lack of capital for growth and expansion. Also, unless the rest of the world's currency is on a gold standard, every nation on earth could demand that America replace their dollars with our gold. Most financial experts understand that we are unlikely to see America return to a gold standard unless all countries do likewise and return to the gold standard.

THE GOLD PRICE INCREASE

From the years 2002 to 2009, there was a steady yearly increase in the price of gold, from $271 an ounce to well over $1,000 an ounce in 2008. The price per ounce has jumped to as high as $1,900 an ounce, and the price of certain coins in gem mint condition was over $2,000 an ounce. Individuals who are bold with stock investments often state that the high gold prices are a bubble set to burst when the economy recovers, while others point out that the global uncertainties are a sure sign that precious metals will continue to fluctuate in value, but remain relatively high throughout the future.

What has caused gold prices to spike as they have over the past years? The progressive price increase began with demand. When other nations such as India and China began to prosper, their demand for gold increased. Central banks in certain nations began to purchase tons of gold as a security measure and a hedge against inflation. Gold also has become a popular investment tool for individual investors.

The U.S. dollar is still considered the world's reserve currency, although it is perilously close to losing that status. Nations are now beginning to extend credit to each other based on their own or other currencies. Historically, when the value of the dollar increases, precious metal values tend to decline. When the dollar value decreases, gold and silver instantly rise along with economic fears.

As America remains stuck in what is being termed "a great recession," the value of the dollar continues to decline, the government prints more money, and people look for something to invest in besides the dollar. When economies are on a downturn, people invest in commodities such as gold because of stability and the increasing value of the metals.

Currently much of the world is in geopolitical and economic upheaval. The Middle East seems to be unraveling. America is dealing with high and unsustainable debt, the European nations are in debt and turmoil, unemployment is high, and citizens are living with economic uncertainty. Banks and investors are using gold and silver as a safety net against inflation and the devaluation of fiat currency. Again, demand means gold prices rise.

WHERE ARE GOLD AND SILVER HEADED?

From a prophetic perspective, in the future the Biblical antichrist will seize control of Egypt, Libya and Ethiopia. The entire prediction reads, *"But he shall have power over the treasures of gold and of silver, and over all the precious things of Egypt: and the Libyans and the Ethiopians shall be at his steps*" (Dan. 11:43). The phrase, "treasures of gold and silver" implies the importance of these two precious metals in the time that the antichrist controls the Middle East. Why would the future Biblical antichrist desire the treasures of gold and silver?

Based on prophetic and practical evidence, let us assume that the antichrist will have an Islamic background. Then we need to understand that Muslims, especially in the Arabian Peninsula, Middle East and Indonesia, invest heavily in gold. This precious metal is very important in Islamic apocalyptic tradition. The Haddith, an Islamic book that provides much information about Mohammad, the founder of Islam, mentions a statement that someone overheard Mohammad saying: "...he heard the Messenger of Allah say: 'A time is certainly coming over mankind in which there will be nothing (left) which will be of use save the dinar.' " (Imam Ahmad ibn Hanbal)

Some Islamic commentators believe that paper currency will fail and the only money used in the last days will be the dinar, which is the currency of ten Islamic countries (Algeria, Bahrain, Iraq, Jordan, Kuwait, Libya, Macedonia, Malaysia, Serbia, Tunisia). In early Islamic history, a gold coin was minted called the dinar. After the collapse of the Ottoman Turkish Empire in 1924, there was a lapse in the Islamic currency as many Muslim-dominated countries began accepting the currency of Western nations. This included the British pound and the American dollar.

Several years ago an Islamic group in West Malaysia began minting a gold dinar. Meetings have been conducted in Egypt and Arabia to discuss the need for Muslims to accept the new coinage as the official coin of the Islamic nations. In brief, many apocalyptic Muslims who hold traditions concerning the last days believe there will be a worldwide economic crisis in which all paper money will be useless. The only money of value will be money minted using gold and silver.

Many speculate this is one reason why the gold and silver prices have risen by so much in a short time. In early 2003 the price of gold and silver was rising; but after the invasion of Iraq, the price increased by about thirty percent. There was no explanation for this, since the stock market was rising, the jobless rate was decreasing, and the economy was improving. Why did this happen? The explanation may be found by exploring who is hoarding the gold and silver.

Intelligence research indicates that Muslims are now telling fellow Muslim businessmen to purchase as much gold as possible and get an edge on the market. Huge amounts of gold would provide enough material to produce large numbers of the thin gold dinars, which can one day be sold to fellow Muslims through the Islamic banking system.

Before you think that this sounds impossible, you may recall that in the 1980s silver increased to fifty dollars an ounce and gold spiked to over eight hundred dollars an ounce. Perhaps you also remember how one businessman in America attempted to control the precious metals market and was stopped by the government. History confirms that when a major economic crisis blankets the world, precious metals such as gold and silver are sought after by investors, businessmen, and private individuals.

GOLD AND SILVER BACKED CURRENCY

It is no secret that there is an interest in eventually having one common global currency. How could this currency be secured if there are many governments using the same currency that would be printed by the International Monetary Fund or a special World Bank? The answer would be to place a gold standard behind the global currency.

In my travels I have heard rumors circulating that are not commonly reported by the national media. Let me share some things that *could* happen in the future, and say why gold and silver (Dan. 11:43) will become significant during the future tribulation.

It is possible that nations such as India, China and Russia may place their own currencies or a new global currency on a gold standard. America would participate in this system, using either gold or perhaps a silver standard to back their currency.

Information from a high ranking person in Europe reveals that the United States has selected ten cities in which to build ten "treasure banks." These banks will be where wealthy individuals can place their physical gold and silver assets, which in return will be used as the financial backing of a United States currency. Instead of "faith in the government" backing the currency, the *people themselves* will hold the key to the backing of currency and the printing of the money.

Gold and silver in storage will be like having ten Fort Knox's scattered across the nation. In exchange for placing the gold and silver in these vaults, small interest payments will be made each year to large investors. If an investor withdraws the precious metals before the signed contract with the bank expires, a penalty will be charged. The metals remain in the vaults as a benefit to both the investor and the bank. In preparation for such a move, I was told that one very wealthy businessman invested over three-hundred-fifty million dollars in the purchase of gold, which he brought from Dubai to the United States for the future purpose of placing it in these special banks.

WHEN GOLD WON'T MATTER

Gold and silver will definitely be part of the early economic control during the first half of what is called the Biblical great tribulation (Matt. 24:21). As the world moves into the latter part of the great tribulation spoken of in the book of Revelation, there will be such cosmic upheavals and natural disasters that food and water will be the most precious commodities, while gold and silver will be useless (Revelation chapter 6).

During the final forty-two months of the great tribulation, all purchasing and selling will be done through the use of a mark on the right hand or forehead, or through the name and special number of the antichrist system which he will establish to control the world's economy (Rev. 13:11-18). During this latter season of world government, the crisis will be one of human survival by any means.

The writer of James had an interesting observation to make concerning the last days and rich men. We read:

> *"Come now, you rich, weep and howl for your miseries that are coming upon you! Your riches are corrupted, and your garments are moth-eaten. Your gold and silver are corroded, and their corrosion will be a witness against you and will eat your flesh like fire. You have heaped up treasure in the last days. Indeed the wages of the laborers who mowed your fields, which you kept back by fraud, cry out; and the*

*cries of the reapers have reached the ears of the Lord of Sabaoth. You
have lived on the earth in pleasure and luxury; you have fattened your
hearts as in a day of slaughter. You have condemned, you have murdered the just; he does not resist you."*

– JAMES 5:1-6 (NKJV)

In this prophetic warning James is rebuking rich men who have
stored up vast amounts of wealth (treasure) for the last days, and at the
same time have abused the employees working for them. These businessmen kept back the wages of their workers, which was forbidden
under God's law. No doubt this was the very law being broken:

*"You shall not oppress a hired servant who is poor and needy, whether
one of your brethren or one of the aliens who is in your land within
your gates. Each day you shall give him his wages, and not let the sun
go down on it, for he is poor and has set his heart on it; lest he cry out
against you to the LORD, and it be sin to you."*

– DEUT. 24:14-15 (NKJV)

The cries of abused and unpaid workers enter into the ears of the
Lord of *Sabaoth* (James 5:4). This is not the Lord of *Sabbath*, as the
Sabbath is the seventh day of the week and refers to the day of rest
(Exod. 16:23). This word Sabaoth is found twice, in Romans 9:29 and
in James 5:4. The word in James is of Hebrew origin and means the
armies of a host of military persons. It is actually a reference to God
Himself who stands up and does battle for His people and, in James 5,
for the poor and unpaid workers!

In the 1611 English translation of the Old Testament, the Hebrew
root of this word is translated as the "Lord of hosts" (Ps. 46:11; 48:8;
59:5; 69:6). James also said these rich men had condemned the righteous and murdered the just (James 5:6). God was preparing to rise up
as a warrior and judge these arrogant men, whose wealth would not
save them in the day of God's judgment and vengeance.

From a prophetic perspective and a future world view, there is
coming a time during the future great tribulation when all of man's
financial investments will be useless, as survival through food and
water will be the primary goal. However, how will things actually be

prior to the gathering together of the saints in heaven—that is, prior to the catching away of true believers, referred to by the apostle Paul in 1 Thessalonians 4:16-17? The answer might surprise you!

CHAPTER 3

The Code of the Last Days of Noah and Lot

"But as the days of Noah were, so also will the coming of the Son of Man be."

– MATTHEW 24:37 (NKJV)

CHRIST HIMSELF INDICATED that the days prior to His return would parallel the days of Noah, whose story is found in the Torah in Genesis. In the well-noted Olivet discourse of Matthew 24, Christ stated that the events prior to Noah's flood would be repeated in the last generation before He would return again. The writer Luke mentions the days of Noah and also Lot as patterns to review in order to understand the many signs that will occur prior to the Messiah's second appearing.

"And as it was in the days of Noah, so it will be also in the days of the Son of Man: They ate, they drank, they married wives, they were given in marriage, until the day that Noah entered the ark, and the flood came and destroyed them all. Likewise, as it was also in the days of Lot: they ate, they drank, they bought, they sold, they planted, they built; but on the day that Lot went out of Sodom it rained fire and brimstone from heaven and destroyed them all. Even so will it be in the day when the Son of Man is revealed."

– LUKE 17:26-30 (NKJV)

After hearing hundreds of messages preached using the days of Lot and Noah as a preview of the days prior to Christ's arrival, it seemed the emphasis was always on the sins of those two time periods and the fact that the judgments came as a sudden surprise to the disobedient people. There is also an emphasis on the fact that the world was destroyed by *water* in Noah's day (Genesis chapter 7) and cities by *fire* in Lot's time (Genesis chapter 19). Something that is often overlooked are the many *activities* occurring on the earth in Noah's time and in Sodom at Lot's time, prior to God striking His swift hand of judgment in both narratives.

PARALLELS OF LOT AND NOAH

Here is a list from both Matthew 24 and Luke 17 of the business and busyness that was happening on a daily basis prior to the wrath of God being poured out:

- Eating

- Drinking

- Marrying Wives

- Given in Marriage

- Selling

- Planting

- Building

In the Genesis stories not much detail is given. Christ gave more detail of the activities than Moses did in his Genesis account. Moses wrote that in Noah's day the earth was wicked (6:5), filled with evil imaginations (6:5), corrupt (6:12) and violent (6:13). In the city of Sodom during the days of Lot, we know there was sexual perversion because we read of young and old men performing acts of sodomy on one another (Ge.n 19). Peter also adds that Lot was vexed daily with the "filthy conversation of the wicked" that grieved Lot's soul (2 Pet.

2:7-8). The prophet Ezekiel added to the list of Sodom's sins when he said:

> *"Look, this was the iniquity of your sister Sodom: She and her daughter had pride, fullness of food, and abundance of idleness; neither did she strengthen the hand of the poor and needy. And they were haughty and committed abomination before Me; therefore I took them away as I saw fit."*
>
> – Ezekiel 16:49-50 (NKJV)

Prophetic expositors point out the many sins that led up to the destruction, and which parallel the times in which we now live. However, there is a "code" that is very obvious, yet often remains concealed under layers of other, more obvious negative happenings. Here is the often-overlooked parallel.

PROSPERITY UNTIL THE DAY COMES

In the earlier list, men who lived during both timeframes were *eating, drinking, building* and *planting*. Doing just these four things requires a steady flow of prosperity among the inhabitants of the land. Also, any man marrying a wife would need a house to raise a family and, in that day, land on which to farm. The overlooked factor was that there seemed to be great prosperity, economic development, and construction occurring up to the very day the water flooded the planet and the fire scorched Sodom and Gomorrah. This emphasis on the prosperity during the times of Noah and Lot is an often overlooked detail when comparing the ancient world to the present society.

Why did Christ emphasize for all believers to watch and pray, lest we be *caught off guard* by His sudden coming? (Matt. 24:43; Mark 13:33). The simple answer is that since we do not *know* the day or the hour of Christ's coming, we could be caught off guard by eating, drinking, drunkenness and abusing others (see Luke 12:45-48). In Luke 12, the servant said in his heart that the Lord was delaying his coming and thus began to live a careless lifestyle.

Let me explain it this way as a minister of the prophetic word. I have observed two different cycles over many years of ministry: the *expectancy* cycle and the *delay* cycle. Anytime a major event transpires—a deadly terrorist attack, a destructive tsunami, a major earthquake, an economic recession, geopolitical upheaval and so on—the informed believers move into the cycle of expectancy. Believers begin to discuss the signs of the times and how the church is so near the return of Christ, based upon newspaper eschatology.

After events settle down, employment figures improve, the economy recovers, no major prophetic events have happened and there are no immediate signs of the return of the Lord, then the *delay cycle* beings to encircle the minds of believers. A mindset of delay places the return of Christ at a later time, another season, or even future generations. These two opposite opinions are motivated by the number and intensity of either negative or positive signs that are found in the ancient Biblical prophecies.

The cycle, especially for Western Christians, is generally tied to the level of national and personal prosperity. When things are going well, people move to the delay cycle. This is significant because Christ told His disciples in the parable of the nobleman to occupy until He comes (Luke 19:13). This word *occupy* is a Greek word meaning *to busy oneself by doing business and trading*. We refer to a person's job as an occupation. The point in the parable is for a believer not to sit back and do nothing but wait for the return of the master; instead, do business until the very day He returns.

Herein we find the "Noah and Lot code." When Christ returns for the believers, life will be moving along in a normal fashion, with building, planting and personal prosperity. Many prophetic students believe the world will practically be falling apart before the Lord returns, and these destructive signs are the trigger of His return. This is partially true, as the signs of famine, pestilence, earthquakes, wars, and rumors of wars are called the birth pains, or the beginning of sorrows according to Matthew 24:8.

These birth pains will intensify and increase. Famines, earthquakes and wars impact the economies, especially in the areas struck by the disaster. However, based on the days of Noah and Lot, before the time of the tribulation, the minds of people will not be on *repentance* but upon *prosperity and life as usual.* In the Biblical examples, the people were so busy with their daily activities, they were ignoring the warning of a righteous man who was building the ark. Lot warned his family that judgment was coming, but his sons-in-law mocked him (Gen. 19:14). I believe this is another reason we are to watch, pray and stay alert, as Jesus will come in a day and an hour that you expect not (Mark 13:32).

SIGNS OF HIS RETURN

Christ made it clear that no one, not even the angels in heaven, know the day and hour of His return (Mark. 13:32). Below is a list based upon what you may understand about end time prophecy signs. Which of these two lists of events is the indicator of Christ's return?

These Signs?	Or These Signs?
Dangerous cosmic activity, such as meteorites	Wonderful signs and discoveries in heaven
Dangerous famine and drought	Lots of rain being poured out in dry places
Marrying, then divorcing your companion	An increase in marriages
Buildings collapsing in earthquakes	Large numbers of buildings being built
Increase in starvation around the world	An overabundance of food in places
Extreme poverty	Extreme prosperity
Food withering in some nations	Food being grown in modern nations

If you chose the list on the left, you are correct. If you selected the list on the right, you are also correct. There will be both negative and dangerous signs along with positive signs and prosperity.

One of the best examples in my lifetime of how quickly people shifted from expecting the imminent return of Christ to delaying the event was the arrival of the year 2000, which you might recall was referred to as Y2K. The theory was that the internal clocks in computers and appliances would turn to 000, which could not be read by computers, and thus anything dependent on computers would fail. The world would be brought to its knees at midnight on the year 2000. The Scriptures that jumped out in this situation were found in Matthew 25—the parable of the ten virgins. *"At midnight, the cry was made, Behold the bridegroom cometh; go ye out to meet him"* (Matt. 25:6). Many around the world anticipated a major collapse of modern civilization or the return of Christ at midnight, so to some this seemed to be a cryptic reference to the Y2K crisis.

The week before the alleged event, churches were packed with concerned believers and sinners alike, wondering if Christ would return at midnight for His chosen ones. When the panic ceased about one minute past midnight, the sinners were back to sinning and the believers were back to their normal lives, relieved that their car, microwave and electrical appliances still worked. The same was true on September 11, 2001 as fear of what else could happen following the attack seized the hearts of many Americans. After the September attack, church attendance was up thirty percent; but within three months, people were back to their normal routines. Any major event tends to swing the pendulum between the extremes of "this is it" to "back to normal."

If Christ were to return when the world is in utter and complete chaos, with collapsing governments, massive global death and persecution, then anyone familiar with the Bible would not only be looking for Christ to return but would be praying that He would hasten His arrival. But when all is well and things return to normal, concern for His return wanes and becomes a secondary thought. This observation helped me understand the following passage:

> *"Knowing this first: that scoffers will come in the last days, walking according to their own lusts, and saying, "Where is the promise of His coming? For since the fathers fell asleep, all things continue as they were from the beginning of creation."*
>
> − 2 PETER 3:3-4 (NKJV)

The scoffing is directed toward those who teach in the promise of Christ's return (John 14:1-3), while the reason for the mocking is that globally and locally, things appear to remain the same. As we would say, life goes on.

The Bible teaches that people will mock prophetic warnings before the judgments of God are released. Prior to the Babylonian captivity, Jeremiah was ridiculed and threatened with death for warning the inhabitants of Jerusalem of the coming famine, invasion and captivity. He sounded the alarm for twenty-three years, in the clamor of much unbelief. The spiritual rumor was that the *prophecy was not matching the prosperity*! Things were going too well for judgment to fall. Of course God would continue to bless the city.

But the Lord said in Jeremiah 22:21, "I spoke to you in your prosperity, but you said, 'I will not hear.' This has been your manner from your youth, that you did not obey My voice." When things go well people tend to forget what got them there.

THE FINAL CHURCH AGE WILL EXPERIENCE PROSPERITY

The book of Revelation was addressed to seven specific churches, all located in an area known as Asia Minor, and was written by the Apostle John around AD 95. These seven churches were located in seven major cities and each name has a specific meaning:

The City	The Reference	Meaning of the City's Name
Ephesus	Rev. 2:1-7	desirable
Smyrna	Rev. 2:8-11	myrrh
Pergamos	Rev. 2:12-17	height or elevation
Thyatira	Rev. 2:18-29	continual sacrifice
Sardis	Rev. 3:1-6	a remnant
Philadelphia	Rev. 3:7-13	brotherly love
Laodicea	Rev. 3:14-22	the rights (rule) of the people

While there are scholars who differ with the following opinion, some have noted and suggested that these seven churches also reveal seven different periods of time throughout church history, from the time of the birth of the church at Pentecost until the climax of the church age. A suggested pattern and time frame is listed here:

THE SEVEN CHURCH AGES

The Church	The Church Age	The Time Frame
Ephesus	The Apostolic Church	AD 32 to 100
Smyrna	The Persecuted Church	100 to 312
Pergamos	The Roman Church	313 to 600
Thyatira	The Dark Ages	600 to 1517
Sardis	The Reformation	1517 to 1700
Philadelphia	The Missions Church	1648 to 21st century
Laodicea	The Lukewarm Church	the present situation

Notice that the seventh church listed in consecutive order by John is the church located in Laodicea. This church was recognized and rebuked by Christ for being lukewarm. When we examine the text further, we discover some interesting statements made by the leadership in this church in Revelation 3:17:

- We are rich

- We are increased with goods

- We have need of nothing

As pointed out in my *Breaking the Apocalypse Code* series, the city of Laodicea was forty miles from Ephesus and was steeped in Greek culture. The city had schools, libraries and a banking center, and it was well off financially and economically. Two famous salves were produced in the city; one was made for the ears and the other for the eyes. Remember that Christ said, "He that has an ear, let him hear" (Rev. 3:22). He commanded the Laodicean believers to anoint their eyes with eye salve (Rev. 3:18), which was a reference to the famous salves acclaimed for their healing properties and produced in the city. Christ said the believers in the church were neither hot nor cold, but were lukewarm (Rev. 3:16).

The lukewarm comment also has an unusual natural parallel to the city. Laodicea's one drawback was the water supply, as water had to be piped into the city. Cold water could come from the abundant supply at Colossae, but by the time it traveled the ten or so miles from the cold springs, it was lukewarm. About six miles away in Hierapolis were hot springs, but that water, too, was lukewarm when it reached Laodicea. If they piped in either the cold or the hot water, it arrived at Laodicea lukewarm. This is why Christ compared the spiritual zeal and commitment of the people in this church to the lukewarm water that would be spewed out of His mouth.

If this seventh church listed by John is a picture of the final church age, then the Scripture reveals the condition of the end time church prior to Christ's gathering of the overcoming saints to heaven. The condition represents a final church that is materially and financially wealthy, increased with many possessions and things, and having all their needs met. This sounds like an exciting, prosperous congregation. However, in this case, the prosperity was preventing them from maintaining the spiritual zeal, fire, and sold-out dedication to Christ. They have possessions without power, wealth without true worship, and prosperity without God's presence!

WHAT THIS REVEALS TO US

In the time of the end, it appears from Scripture that the world and the church will have material wealth and prosperity. There has never been a generation in world history such as ours, where technology and knowledge have increased so greatly that individuals can develop ideas and inventions that create great wealth. The challenge for us is to understand that the combination of prosperity, as in the days of Noah and Lot, and the pattern of the final church age, as in the possession of great wealth, holds both a blessing and a curse. For those who are obedient to God's covenant, it is a blessing; but for the disobedient it is a curse.

The wealth of believers is given by the hand of the Almighty to be a blessing to both the believer and those to whom they minister. This includes the widows, the orphans, the poor, and those who are lost without a covenant relationship with Christ. If believers give of their tithe and offerings, and properly distribute the resources, then many souls are reached for eternity.

The curse of prosperity falls upon people when greed takes control. Greed takes possession of the person's soul and causes people to become selfish and self-serving. They will even abuse other people for their own personal gain.

One warning in the code of Noah and Lot is this: the material wealth and goods that we own cannot be taken with us once we depart this life. The material possessions in Lot's day were consumed in the flames of the city, while in Noah's time, water covered the homes. This left both Noah and Lot having to search out a new land and dwelling place once the smoke settled and the flood waters receded.

The second warning is this: do not allow the success of life and business prosperity to blind you into thinking that the Lord's coming will be delayed because you mistakenly think He must return in times of chaos and not prosperity. When your eyes are on prosperity, they are moved away from the *parousia*, a Greek word for the Lord's *coming* (1 Thess. 2:19; 3:13; 4:15). It was Christ who warned about the cares of life and the deceitfulness of riches (Mark 4:19), and how that through overindulgence, the day (of Christ's return) would come upon a person unaware (Luke 21:34).

A third warning is that things will immediately change the day of Christ's return. Peace will be replaced by war and prosperity by persecution and pestilence. In Noah's time, all things continued as normal until the rain began to pelt the ground, and in Lot's time when fire—possibly volcanic—began raining down upon Sodom (Gen. 19:24). The people did not know what was coming *until the day* the judgments unfolded (Matt. 24:38-39).

As believers, we must use our resources to reach the lost around the globe in the time that we have remaining. Scripture tells us that the gospel of the kingdom will be preached in all the world as a witness to the nations, and then the end will come (Matthew 24:14). Using your resources to help spread the gospel ensures both an earthly blessing and a heavenly reward, as financial resources are needed to reach nations with the glorious gospel of Christ.

Future financial increase that is in the earth until the return of the Messiah *should and must be* the war chest of the believer, and it must be tapped into in order to bring help, relief and deliverance to those in need.

THE FOUR BLESSINGS FOR NOAH

There is one more aspect to this Noah code that is overlooked. For believers, there is a great hope in the time of the end. We know that in Noah's day, the imaginations of men were evil (Gen 6:5), the earth was filled with violence (Gen. 6:11), and immorality was rampant (Gen. 6:4). What is seldom taught by prophetic ministers are the four blessings that Noah experienced before the flood came, and these blessings should parallel the four blessings that we as believers can experience before the coming day of the Lord.

1. WE WILL PREACH UNTIL THE DAY THAT CHRIST RETURNS

Many attempts have and still are being made to pass laws that limit free speech and persecute Christians in North America and other Western nations. This causes many to believe the day will come when liberal leaders will pass laws to shut the mouths of evangelical Christians. However, Noah had about one hundred years (compare Gen. 5:32 with Gen. 7:6) to warn his generation before the flood came. The Apostle Peter wrote:

> *"And spared not the old world, but saved Noah the eighth person, a preacher of righteousness, bringing in the flood upon the world of the ungodly."*
>
> – 2 PETER 2:5

According to 1 Peter 3:20, the Almighty was waiting for Noah to complete the ark before He released the universal flood upon mankind.

Despite the fact that in one hundred years, Noah was unable to convince anybody that destruction was coming, and despite the fact that people mocked his warnings, he continued to warn them up to the day he entered the ark and God closed the door.

The reason I can say with assurance that, despite opposition against the Gospel, we will continue to preach is because of the promise given by Christ in Matthew 24:14:

> *"And this gospel of the kingdom shall be preached in all the world for a witness unto all nations; and then shall the end come."*
>
> – MATT. 24:14

The church is not defined by a building, as the first century church met mostly in homes (Acts 2:46; 5:42; Rom. 16:5; Col. 4:15). Neither is the church a certain denomination or branch of Christianity that some might consider the exclusive Body of Christ on the earth. The word *church* in Greek is *ekklesia* and refers to an assembly of called out ones. Thus the church is the individual believers from around the world whose names are recorded in the Book of Life (Phil 4:3; Rev. 3:5).

The great promise given to the church is that, because it is built upon the rock, or the foundation of Christ, then the "gates of hell shall not prevail against it" (Matt. 16:18). The word prevail means to overpower. The adversaries of Christianity have fought the church but will never overpower this living, thriving spiritual body on earth. So the first bit of good news is that the church will be preaching up until the day of the Lord's return.

2. WE WILL REACH OUR FAMILIES

Lot failed to convince his daughters and sons-in-law that Sodom was under judgment (Gen. 19:14), and he even lost his wife when she looked back (Gen. 19:26). Noah, on the other hand, was successful in bringing his entire family into the ark for protection from the flood (Gen. 6 and 7). Noah had such grace and favor in the eyes of the Lord that God gave him the privilege of seeing his entire family saved.

Just as Noah was obedient to seek God's will first, and God honored him by bringing his entire household to safety, we must seek first the kingdom of God and believe that the same favor will be upon us as we lead all of our family, including our children and their children, into the kingdom of God before the very time of the end and the rise of the future antichrist. Our promise should be the same words spoken to the jailor when God visited the prison with an earthquake, *"And they said, Believe on the Lord Jesus Christ, and thou shalt be saved, and thy house"* (Acts 16:31).

The fulfillment of this promise may require years of deep intercession and tears as we pray against satanic opposition, spiritual blindness and dullness of hearing that infects the understanding of many. However, we should believe that, as Noah led his family into the Ark, we will lead our family into the Kingdom!

3. WE WILL BE ABLE TO COMPLETE OUR END TIME DESTINIES

Noah was six hundred years of age the day it began to rain for forty days and nights (Gen. 7:6). Noah's assignment was to build an ark and collect animals for the long ride on the flood waters. He finished his assignment in every aspect and was successful to complete each detail on time. Many believers know that they have promises of destinies yet unfulfilled, and some believe that, based on current events and the economic conditions of the earth, Jesus will return before they can complete their calling.

Throughout your life the adversary will make attempts to prevent your progress, block your movement, and stop your destiny. On several occasions the enemies of Christ attempted to kill Him, but in each case they were unsuccessful because "His hour had not yet come" (John 7:30; 8:20).

Another example was the apostle John. According to the early church father Tertullian, John was boiled in oil in Rome in a large coliseum and survived, causing the entire coliseum to turn to Christ. To remove his influence from the public arena, John was banished to the isle of Patmos where he could have died, but was later released after the death of the evil emperor Domitian.

John had a destiny to fulfill. Christ had told His twelve disciples that there were some who would not taste death until they saw the Son of man coming in the kingdom (Luke 9:27). John saw the kingdom in a vision he recorded called the apocalypse, or the book of Revelation. Thus, he could not die until his assignment was completed.

We should all pray that none of us will experience a premature departure from this life so that we can fulfill all that the Lord instructs us to do. It is written of Joshua that he left "nothing undone of all the Lord commanded Moses" (Josh 11:15). Just as Esther came to the kingdom for such a time as this (Est. 4:14), you arrived on the planet in this season for a specific purpose of influencing others for the Gospel and warning them of things to come before they occur. Your mission is greater than your opposition.

4. WE WILL FINISH STRONG AND NOT IN DEFEAT

As the ark rose above the waters and only eight souls survived the destruction, they finished strong and not defeated. Finishing the race strong should be the goal of each believer. When Paul was preparing for his beheading in Rome, he wrote his last letter to Timothy saying;

"I have fought a good fight, I have finished my course, I have kept the faith."

– 2 TIMOTHY 4:7

Paul's ministry had caused uprisings in major cities, sending him to prison on several occasions. His faith had been challenged, yet he never backed down. He had run his leg of the race and finished the course, preparing to pass the baton to his spiritual son Timothy. Paul finished strong. We will finish strong.

CHAPTER 4

Parabolic Principles of Financial Growth and Blessing

WHEN WE IN the 21ˢᵗ century quote scriptural promises from the New Testament, some often think the words are ancient and the promises outdated because we live in a different culture with a different lifestyle. However, consider the basic New Testament methods of earning income, and notice the parallels to our own contemporary society.

The beautiful and famed Mediterranean Sea runs along the western coastline of Israel. In Christ's time, it was a source of shipping and trade, with major ports in Joppa and Caesarea handling imports and exports of goods and agricultural products from Israel. Another body of water—actually a large lake—is the Sea of Galilee, which was the site of the fishing industry. Dotted around the lake were numerous cities and villages where the young men often followed in their family's tradition of working in the fishing industry. A New Testament example is Zebedee and his sons, James and John, who were mending nets when Christ called them into the ministry (Matt. 4:21-22).

The central region of Israel was the site for farming and agriculture. Jerusalem, the spiritual capital of the nation, was noted for natural olive trees. When the olives from the Mount of Olives were crushed, the first pressing was used for lighting the Menorah in the Temple.

In Bethlehem the fields were known for both barley and wheat, two of the primary grains grown in Israel. The rugged land in and around Hebron was the center of the grape and wine industry, as the best grapes in the nation were grown in the hills of Hebron. In the time of Moses, when the twelve men returned from spying out the land, they carried poles with huge vines of grapes to demonstrate the abundance of the land (Num. 13:23).

Pomegranate and fig trees also covered the land. Scattered throughout the towns and cities were carpenters, or stone masons. The majority of buildings constructed in the time of Christ were made from either natural stones stacked upon one another and cemented in place, or from limestone hand cut in quarries.

Other minor jobs included net mending, pottery making, salt mining, and even cooking.

Despite the fact that our global society is linked by high technology, the industries listed above are still part of the income base for many individuals in nations around the world, especially in smaller towns and villages scattered throughout Mexico, Europe, Asia and third world nations. Fishing, shipping and trade, farming, vineyards and fruit trees, grain fields, and carpentry are all income-producing jobs in America. Thus, beyond the industries that deal with technological breakthroughs, the basic needs of people—food, shelter and clothes—remain the same.

TROUBLES THAT AFFECTED THE ECONOMY

In the New Testament era, six negative circumstances impacted the various industries, costing jobs and resulting in a great loss of income.

Droughts and famines would destroy an entire harvest, especially wheat and barley, which were two of the staple foods for the entire nation. Occasionally pestilence, such as locusts and plagues, would strike the land and destroy young plants and certain food supplies. The region was not prone to flooding, as the only main water source for the nation was the Jordan River. However, extreme rain would cause difficulties, just as floods today can destroy property and crops.

Warring armies from surrounding nations would seize towns and cities, often cutting off the food and water supply to the inhabitants, and thus causing starvation. Prior to the destruction of Jerusalem, the Romans laid siege on the city and the inhabitants were unable to leave the city or receive any food for months.

At times, mobs would attack a village or a home and take food or any possession they desired from the homeowner. During times of famine, roving bands of men would break into houses searching for food that might be hidden in a home. These mobs would rob, plunder, steal, rape, and at times burn down the home or the town once they completed their raids.

Another problem was high taxes. At various times throughout history—and especially under the Roman empire—taxes and other duties caused a heavy burden on the citizens.

Many of these same challenges are still present over two thousand years later. Drought, floods, war, pestilence, and civil disruptions are still occurring around the world and causing heartache and economic troubles in the areas where they occur.

We cannot stop an earthquake, a tornado, or a hurricane from striking. We cannot keep floods from washing away farmland and property. In some nations, war and civil disobedience (as we have seen in Greece) cause more economic crisis, especially for local business owners. Just ask those business owners who lost weeks of income or dealt with property damage during the "occupy Wall Street" protests.

In the gospels, Christ told the story of a vineyard, which can be viewed as a parable with practical application for our own financial and business success. I call these practical applications "parabolic principles of success in finance and business."

THE STORY CONCEALED IN PARABLES

In Matthew 20:1, Christ compared the kingdom of heaven to workers being hired in a vineyard:

> *"For the kingdom of heaven is like unto a man that is a householder, which went out early in the morning to hire laborers into his vineyard."*

The listener was certainly aware of life in a vineyard, as vineyards were (and still are) a part of the agriculture in Israel. The Jewish audience would have been familiar with the concept of hiring workers to labor in a vineyard; thus the comparison of the kingdom of heaven with a person who hired workers and gave them a specific wage for their labor.

The one parable that reveals some insight into the parallels between caring for a vineyard and being successful in both business and life is found in Luke 13:6-9. In this parable a fig tree is planted within a vineyard:

"He spake also this parable; A certain man had a fig tree planted in his vineyard; and he came and sought fruit thereon, and found none. Then said he unto the dresser of his vineyard, Behold, these three years I come seeking fruit on this fig tree, and find none: cut it down; why cumbereth it the ground?

And he answering said unto him, Lord, let it alone this year also, till I shall dig about it, and dung it: And if it bear fruit, well: and if not, then after that you shall cut it down."

The above narrative, called a parable, is a story that illustrates a moral, financial, or religious lesson; thus it is a lesson within a story. Christ often spoke in parables. While opinions vary on the division of the stories within the parables, Christ spoke about fifty parables in the New Testament. Each parable was based upon facts, people, subjects, or incidents that the people of His day were familiar with and could relate to in a practical manner. He spoke of a fig tree (Luke 13:6-9), a net (Matt. 13:47-48), a marriage (Matt. 9:15), the harvest (Matt. 9:37) a Samaritan (Luke 10:30-37), a shepherd (John 10:1-6); a lost sheep, a lost coin and a lost son (Luke 15:4-32); slaves (Matt. 24:45-51); and virgins (Matt. 25;1-12), to name a few.

The same practical lessons that Christ was teaching the people of His day are the same lessons we must learn and follow in the 21st century. Certain parables reveal details concerning Christ's return (Matthew 25). They reveal specific second coming insights that we must understand as we draw closer to the return of the Messiah. Other parables reveal practical applications for daily living or financial secrets concealed within the story. Such is the case when we look at the process of planting, growing, and harvesting from a vineyard.

THE VINEYARD APPLICATION

Concealed in the methods used to plant, grow, and harvest grapes from a vineyard are hidden the principles of planting, preparing, and prospering in the area of finances and business. Let's look at five principles for growing and caring for a vineyard.

The first and basic law of growth is to *plant*. There is no harvest until the seeds are first planted in the soil. For a successful vineyard a *good site* must be selected, including an open field with no shade trees that would block sunlight. There must be plenty of open space where air can reach the vines. Ridge tops are excellent as this provides needed drainage. The vines are to be planted in straight rows and evenly spaced at the proper depths.

For *protection*, stone walls were placed around the vines to prevent small animals from entering the vineyard and eating the young buds, thus destroying the future harvest. In Hebron, large nets are used to cover the entire vineyard, thus preventing birds from settling on the vines and damaging the plants.

The third phase is that the vines must be *fertilized* to assist in the growth process. In vineyards, it is common to see no results the first year. But in a few years, with proper care and nourishment of the vines, the planter will enjoy a grape harvest.

The fourth and very important process is to mark any branch that may die, and in the off season, to *cut the dead branches* from the vine. Any dead branch will sap the life from the other living branches, and eventually cause the vine not to produce fruit.

Finally, the most enjoyable process is the *harvesting* of the grapes, which occurs in Israel between August and October on the normal cycle.

If we take the five-fold process from planting to harvesting of a vineyard and apply it practically to our lives, we can see how the same five steps are important in the development of your own business or job growth and financial security.

1. PLANT IN THE RIGHT LOCATION

Vineyards must be planted in the area of other vines for the purpose of cross-pollination from the other vines. The pollination process is necessary to produce the young buds that eventually mature and produce fruit.

How does that apply to us? A person cannot be successful by becoming a loner and living in isolation, away from other people. Even Christ revealed that "men would give to your bosom" (Luke 6:38). God uses men and women to open the doors of opportunity for others. Isolation separates you from opportunity, as people need people, and people hire other people. While it is God who opens the door of opportunity, you must be available to walk through it.

When it comes to the location for a business, or for that matter a church, you must be planted in the right area. Take into consideration the community needs you are trying to meet and the assignments you intend to accomplish. I have lived in Cleveland, Tennessee for over thirty years and have seen businesses remain the entire time, while others have risen and fallen. In two particular locations, restaurants have come and gone, and not one new owner has maintained a business there for longer than two years. The primary reason was location. Another problem is advertising. One restaurant purchased a billboard at the turn exit. By the time you read the billboard, you passed the exit! Simply placing the advertising a few miles before the exit ramp could have increased business for the restaurant. Location is important.

The same is true for a church. Just because land is cheaper in a certain part of town does not mean that is the best place to build. Many of the older downtown churches have few active members, as the church was built before the town grew. In those days, people might have walked to church. Today there might be minimal parking available for attendees as the city built around the church. It might be necessary to park quite a distance away and walk to the facility. This would be fine for young people, but it can be a hindrance if most of your congregation is over seventy years of age.

What are your long term goals and visions for your business, church, or even your family? If you open a shop in a mini-mall where most of the other businesses have closed, then you can just about guarantee that your business will not succeed, unless your product or activity (such as a gym) has high demand and an already-established and loyal clientele. Use wisdom when planting your business. Don't open an ice factory in Alaska, or a pork rib restaurant in Israel. Not long ago a grocery store sign was circulating on the Internet that read, "Get your Hanukkah hams here!" Hanukah is a Jewish celebration and Jews don't eat pork. So don't make that kind of mistake.

If you are going to plant a small business or a church, plant in the right area to meet the need. An inner city church must be in the inner city, a day care center must be in a convenient place and a safe environment, and parking needs must be taken into consideration.

2. PROTECT WHAT YOU INITIATE

I refer to this as "hedging things in." Hedging is a term used by investors to limit their losses. For example, with life insurance, you purchase it knowing that one day you will die and your family will receive the insurance money, while the insurance company is speculating that you will live a long life and keep paying premiums.

Just as birds pluck young blossoms in a vineyard, and foxes gnaw and damage vines, so will sickness and accidents impact you in a negative economic manner. Just as a vineyard requires protection for production, it is also important for you to protect your personal and business investment. The first principle is, do not go into extreme personal or business debt that is unsustainable and un-payable. Professional money managers suggest that a person should set aside at least six months of operating expenses to cover their bills in the event of a job loss or emergency. You want your business, ministry, or home to remain intact should you be unable to perform your job duties for a period of time.

In a vineyard, not all of the young vines will survive. Some will fail to grow and produce fruit. This is normal, just as not every investment in the secular world produces the anticipated profit. When a vine-dresser sees vines that have died, he simply replaces the dying with a new living vine. He does not become angry, shake his fist and curse the ground, or walk away from the other plants that will produce in the future.

One of the most important times to protect vines is during cross pollination and when the young buds appear. In the early stages of opening a small business, investing, or planting a church or ministry, there will be unexpected hindrances and expenses. At times there will be opposition from unusual sources. From a ministry perspective, there is usually spiritual opposition in some form.

Part of your strategy is to have other options available—a plan B—if things do not work out as planned. The first vehicle invented by Henry Ford had a two-cylinder ethanol engine and four bicycle wheels. It was called a quadracycle, and it had one major problem—no reverse gears. Ford also had to cut a larger hole in the wall to get the car out.

Thomas Edison was a master inventor who spent two million dollars on one invention and never developed what he wanted. He also picked up invention ideas that other inventors started on but dropped. He had to correct thousands of his own creative failures before he found the right combinations for light bulbs and batteries.

Neither Ford nor Edison stopped because of failure or mistakes, but continued to press forward and develop other plans that eventually succeeded. Instead of considering his mistake a failure, Ford learned from the mistake, and today Ford Motor Company is the top manufacturer of pick-up trucks in America. When something failed, both men simply reached out for another direction while remaining focused on the assignment.

Often investors diversify their investments to ensure that if some fail, others will succeed. This principle is found in a statement by the wise teacher Solomon:

> "Cast thy bread upon the waters: for thou shall find it after many days. Give a portion to seven, and also to eight; for thou knowest not what evil shall be upon the earth. If the clouds be full of rain, they empty

themselves upon the earth: and if the tree falls toward the south, or toward the north, in the place where the tree falls, there it shall be."

– ECCL. 11:1-3

After Adam's spiritual fall in the garden, God informed him that, "In the sweat of thy face shalt thou eat bread..." (Gen.3:19). This refers to Adam working among the thorns and the ground to produce a harvest of food. Bread is also a metaphor used to identify the type of work a person does to "bring in the bread," or the income for the family. A husband is often called the "bread winner," meaning that he is generally responsible for bringing in the income and provision.

Casting your bread upon the water seems odd, because when a loaf of bread is thrown on water, it eventually becomes soggy and bloated with water. It will either sink or gradually separate into pieces. In ancient days, bread was an important food supply when traveling by ship. Because of the water and moisture, loaves were often covered with a wax–like coating that prevented water or moisture from allowing the bread to become wet and deteriorate. If a ship wrecked at sea, these loaves could float on the waves and eventually a current could carry the bread to shore. Thus by casting your bread upon the water, it would return on the current and the flow of the waves.

Solomon's instruction to give a portion to seven or to eight can be understood in modern terminology as "do not put all your eggs in one basket." In other words, spread out your investment by diversification. Instead of purchasing stock in one company, invest in several solid corporations.

Notice the phrase "for you know not what evil shall be upon the earth." Global troubles cause markets to rise and fall overnight, and any sudden disruption—such as a national uprising, a natural disaster, a terrorist attack, a tsunami in Japan, or a Gulf disaster in Louisiana—suddenly alters the economic stability of national and global corporations. It is always the *unexpected evil* that lurks in the shadows and appears like a crouching lion waiting for its prey that disrupts your own economic stability. This is one reason that being released from excessive debts and having your bills paid in advance can be a life saving strategy in event of a major crisis or downturn.

3. FERTILIZING FOR FRUITFUL INCREASE

Over a period of time, natural soil can lose important nutrients. A plant needs elements from the air—such as carbon, hydrogen and oxygen—to grow. However, fertilizer contains other mineral nutrients such as nitrogen, phosphorus, and potassium that plants need for growth. If these nutrients are missing in soil, a plant will not grow properly. Fertilizing the soil helps the plant to soak up these elements needed for proper growth.

From a practical application, the idea of fertilizing speaks of both growing your business and of adding other avenues of income to your present income. This could include developing creative ideas that generate money, selling items of value for a profit, or using your own personal gifts to create an income flow.

For many years of my ministry, my only source of income was from traveling and preaching in rural churches. In 1986 we organized a 501(c)3 called the Voice of Evangelism Outreach, Inc. From that moment, a board of directors placed my wife and me on salaries. From the initiation of the ministry until this day, all resource materials, including books, CDs, and DVDs are all owned by the Voice of Evangelism. I receive no personal income or royalties from material sold on television, through the magazine, or in conferences, as all income is used for ministry.

In the early 1990s, I discovered that God gave me a gift for songwriting. I began to write songs and have been blessed to have around forty different songs recorded by such individuals as Mike Purkey, Karen Wheaton, Judy Jacobs, John Starnes, Gold City Quartet, The McKamey's, and others. When a song is recorded, the writer receives a royalty once the song is placed on a CD, DVD, played on television or radio, or printed in a book. Imagine my surprise when I received a royalty check for one song for over four thousand dollars!

From age eighteen, I began writing books and have written over sixty books for the ministry, without receiving any income for my personal time or work. Several years ago I was approached about contracting with a major Christian publisher, and I now have a contract to write books for them. They pay me a writer's advance for writing the books, and they print and distribute them in stores across America and around the world. While all royalties from the sale of the books go directly into the Voice of Evangelism ministry, the advance for writing the books is a *second stream* of income. I also have been blessed to have invented some things and have received occasional royalties from certain inventions. None of these additional sources of income have pulled me away from my ministry assignments, yet each has assisted my family with additional income.

Do you possess special abilities and gifts that can be used to bring additional income into your life? There may be areas that you are unaware of and talents or gifts you have never considered. At times the simplest concepts become the most successful ideas. When you can meet others' needs by bringing joy, knowledge, or health, then your talent or gift can bring income to you.

4. PRUNE THE DEAD WEIGHT

I mentioned that dead branches will eventually pull life and strength from living ones. Thus the lifeless nonproductive branch becomes a liability to the living branches.

Nearly every business, organization and church will eventually encounter both living branches and dead branches—or productive and nonproductive projects. Know when to cut your losses and either close or sell anything that is draining the life and money from the productive side of the organization.

Even people can drain the life (and sometimes customers and money) from a business. The person who produces no fruit always offers excuses for why they are unable to perform productively. They have an excuse for why they are always late to work, why they cannot return from lunch on time, or why they are talking around the coffee machine when they should be answering the phones.

Two mistakes are made in business and ministry. The first is to hire family, just for the sake of giving them a job. Always consider their work ethic before hiring for the sole reason that they are related to the owner or the pastor. Relatives sometimes think they can be held to a lower standard than other employees, and family members can be more difficult to fire once they are hired.

The second mistake is to keep an employee who is a dead branch and cannot or will not do the job. If you have a complainer, an employee who cannot get along with others, or a lazy person on staff, their emotional instability and negative attitude will drain the life out of the other workers. It is better to pay a higher wage to one capable and determined worker, than to provide lower pay for two workers who have a difficult time getting the job done.

Even volunteers can cause trouble. Ministries and churches depend upon volunteers for particular work assignments, and sometimes they can become territorial. There have been times in our ministry when a volunteer's attitude became competitive, selfish and prideful. Sometimes they had a hidden agenda or a negative attitude that caused a wedge of contention between them and others. Remember, a staff member or volunteer is representing you, the CEO, the company director or the pastor. It is better to remove a few contentious people from positions than to allow them to corrupt the dedicated and effective employees and volunteers who obediently follow instructions and perform their task with dedication, honor, and integrity.

Remember, just like a dead vine, what doesn't produce will kill the fruit. Pruning includes purging the wrong thinking, the negative attitudes, and the wrong people that surround you.

5. TIME TO HARVEST

One significant principle that operates in both the spiritual and secular world is that we all reap whatever we sow (Gal. 6:7). The seed planted today is the future harvest gathered tomorrow. Thoughts today become actions tomorrow; dreams today become destinies of the future. Harvesting produce from lands and vines requires work, and the fruit of your labors must be gathered in the time of the harvest.

Grains, grapes, olives and figs all mature but do not harvest themselves. Machines reap the grains, other types of equipment move through groves shaking the small olives from olive trees, and reapers gather grapes from the vines. In Israel grains and fruits are harvested at different seasons of the year. Barley is gathered in the spring, wheat in early summer, and grapes in the late summer and early fall.

For a church or ministry, the fruit of labor is represented by the individual souls and families who are won to Christ and impacted with the gospel. Paul spoke of "fruit abounding to your (heavenly) account" (Phil. 4:17). James taught that God waits patiently for the "precious fruit of the earth" (James 5:7), meaning the souls of mankind that become ripe for harvesting for eternal life after hearing the gospel.

For those investing, the fruit of your labor is the return from your investment. If you rent property, when renters bring you a check they are bringing you the fruit of your labor that you spent providing them housing. For a car salesperson, the commission from the sale of a vehicle is the fruit of your labor. A person who works using their hands, mind, or communication gifts should never be embarrassed, ashamed, or intimidated when rewarded for their work, as this is the method used to bring income for your family and personal needs. The check you receive is the fruit from your efforts. With this fruit reward, you must also take seeds from the fruit and plant them again for a future harvest. This can be done through supporting charities, feeding programs, ministries, or being a blessing to others. By helping others, the door of blessing is opened for another future increase in your life.

"Who then is a faithful and wise servant, whom his lord hath made ruler over his household, to give them meat in due season?"

– MATT. 24:45

IT TAKES TIME TO GROW ANYTHING

From seed planting to harvesting requires patience, as the process involves time. Time is often viewed as an adversary, as we each are given a certain amount each day and an assigned amount for a lifetime. When we plant it takes rain, sunshine, and time to bring a harvest. When building a church it takes prayer, preaching, personal ministry, and time to build a congregation. In business, it takes wise decisions, hard work, and time to bring in a steady clientele. As time turns to days and weeks, it is patience that enables a person to wait, trusting for and expecting a good outcome.

The Almighty, however, has a unique ability to manipulate time and speed up the process of harvest. For example, in John chapter 2, at the wedding of Canaan, Christ took six pots of water and supernaturally turned the water into wine. If a person were to desire a harvest of fresh grape juice, it would require pruning the vines, watering the vineyard (or lots of rain), then harvesting the grapes, crushing them, and collecting the grape juice (also called wine in the New Testament era). In about eight months, you could have six large stone pots from your grape harvest. Christ, however, instantly removed the *time element* required to grow, harvest, and crush the grapes.

Consider a second miracle, the feeding of the five thousand men, plus women and children (Matt. 14:21). What would be required, and what amount of time needed, to prepare fish sandwiches for this many people at an evangelistic event? Perhaps you could rent several hundred boats and hire out hundreds of bakeries, and in a few days come up with the amount of bread and fish needed to host a large outdoor picnic. But Christ prayed over two fish and five loaves of bread and supernaturally multiplied the fish and bread to feed over five thousand people.

An event that would have taken a restaurant owner much money and many days to accomplish was classified as a miracle when Christ removed the time element using the seed of a little to produce the harvest of a lot! These two narratives illustrate how needs can be met when God alters the amount of time normally needed to accomplish a task.

GOD CAN MANIPULATE TIME

Three words in Scripture reveal how God manipulates time. In Ephesians 5:16 we are told to "redeem the time." To *redeem* in this reference means to *rescue from the loss*. If a church is about to close, a business is about to fold or your finances are about to collapse, to redeem the church, business or finances would mean there is an intervention that rescues it from the possible loss.

We see this when individuals enter a redemptive covenant with Christ. After many years of emotional, physical and spiritual abuse and manipulation through sin, the power of redeeming grace and faith brings a restoration and the believer makes up for those wasted years.

The second word is in Joel 2:25, where we read that God will "restore the years." This word restore refers to making amends or making up for the loss. Restoration occurs after something has been lost or is in ruin. When ancient Israel was taken into Babylonian captivity and Jerusalem was in ruins and total destruction, God promised the Hebrews a total restoration from destruction and a blessing to be returned to the land. Loss and devastation for a believer is never permanent. Just ask Job who lost his wealth, ten children, and his health; yet years later, he was blessed with ten more children, double the wealth, and a restoration of his health (see Job 42).

A wonderful passage in Habakkuk 3:2 reads that God will "revive the years." To revive something is to *keep it alive*. When Abraham was told at age seventy-five that he would father a son, twenty-four years later at age ninety-nine he was childless and his wife Sarah was barren. But God kept His promise alive by reviving the bodies of Abraham and Sarah, who at age ninety, gave birth to a son named Isaac (Gen. 21:1-5).

This is one reason why it is important to trust God in the area of finances and financial security for your daily needs and future plans. God's ability to manipulate time should encourage us to understand that He is able to bring results faster than expected and restore losses and remove hindrances.

GOD CAN MANIPULATE NATURAL LAWS

The natural law of gravity causes a heavy piece of iron to sink in water. In 2 Kings 6:6, a man was chopping wood with a borrowed ax head. The heavy head slipped off the handle and sunk in the depths of a river. The man cried out to the prophet Elisha, who through an act of faith caused the ax head to float to the surface where it was snatched up by the appreciative wood chopper! If men can take iron from the earth, melt it, and form panels to build a floating battleship, then certainly God can reverse the law of gravity and cause iron to float.

The law of gravity was also altered when Christ came to His disciples walking on the water of the Sea of Galilee (Matt. 14:29). In the New Testament era, the normal mode of transportation was walking or riding an animal such as a donkey or a camel. But in the book of Acts, Phillip was preaching a revival in Samaria, but God needed him to minister to a man from Ethiopia. The Lord transported Phillip without the use of walking or riding an animal, by supernaturally transporting him from one location to another (Acts 8:27-39).

A third example of altering the natural laws was when God extended daylight for Joshua, thus enabling Israel to defeat an opposing tribe in battle (Josh. 10:13). In the future, God will break all of the natural laws by resurrecting the righteous dead and changing the physical bodies of the living, at an event called the catching away or the gathering together (1 Thess. 4:16-17; Eph. 1:9-10; 1 Cor. 15:51-52).

After Communism collapsed, I was invited to minister in the largest, eight thousand seat hall in Sofia, Bulgaria. I was unaware that the Russians had cut off fuel to Bulgaria and there was a massive shortage throughout the nation. On the final day, we ate lunch with the head Bishop of the unregistered church. As his van was coming off a snowy mountain road, he realized his vehicle was out of fuel. The motor stopped and he was gliding down the roads, using the emergency brake to slow us down. We were asked to pray for a miracle.

I began thinking about Christ's miracle of the multiplication of the loaves and fishes. I knew this was a serious need and only the Lord could multiply fuel in an empty tank. As we prayed, suddenly the Bishop struck the dash with his hand and the gas gauge moved. He then cranked the vehicle and the engine fired up. We drove over twenty miles and the engine stopped at the Bishop's house, where he had a container of fuel.

This does not mean we should ask for fuel when we can *pay* for fuel. In ancient Israel the Hebrew nation was given manna six days a week for forty years, and lived under a cloud by day and a fire by night (Deut. 8:16; Num. 9:16). There was no food or protection from the heat and the cold; thus God provided for the wandering Hebrews for an entire generation! However, once Israel crossed the Jordan River, grain fields provided food in the land and the heavenly manna ceased after the people, "ate the corn of the land" (Josh 5:12). Israel could no longer walk out of their tents and see food all around them (manna). Now, the seeds would be planted and harvested through the works of their hands.

On several occasions, Christ and His disciples were caught in the midst of terrible storms. The description is, "the ship was covered with waves" (Matt. 8:24), "the ship was tossed with waves" (Matt. 14:24), and "they were in jeopardy" (Luke 8:22). We read, "and a great wind-storm arose, and the waves beat into the boat, so that it was already filling" (Mark 4:37). These waves beat against the ship. The Greek word for beat is *epiballo*, and the image is throwing an iron ball at something until you weaken it and it breaks.

Yet, with waves covering a ship and the boat filled with water, the ship did not sink! Boats filled with water sink; yet God broke the normal pattern for a sinking ship and held up the ship with Christ and His disciples in it! The real secret is in the spoken words of Christ in Mark 4:35 when He said, "Let us go over to the other side (of the lake). When Christ gave the command, "Let us go over…" then there was no way they could go *under* for going *over!*

GOD'S LAWS ARE SUPERIOR TO NATURAL LAWS

Christ said it "rains upon the just and the unjust" (Matt. 5:45), meaning trouble comes to both the righteous and the unrighteous. Destructive hurricanes and tornados have ripped neighborhoods apart, leaving a sinner's house intact and a saint's house in ruins, or visa-versa. At times death struck, leaving a sinner in grief and leaving a saint in tears. There is no explanation for why this happens, other than storms have no conscience and do not discriminate against religion, race, or gender. However, Christ rebuked dangerous storms and God heard, preventing premature death. By using the authority He gave us, we can also pray against storms and ask God to manipulate natural laws.

In 2011, I was hosting a mentoring institute at the T.L. Lowery Global Foundation Center in our home town of Cleveland, Tennessee. There were about 225 people in the facility. Terrible tornados had struck Alabama, and according to the news, a possible F-4 tornado was coming toward Cleveland. While we were there, my wife called from home to give us the warning and recommended that we take action now. The wind was already bouncing cars and there was no place for us to go for additional security. I called the people for prayer and told them we must pray against any storm coming toward us.

Watching from the window, I saw the dark clouds swirling. I thought about the story of Christ in the boat, rebuking the storm, when suddenly I saw an open vision of Moses seeing the Red Sea part. I ran to the front and told Mark Casto, who was praying with the group, "Command the tornado to split like the Red Sea!" The entire group began to pray with such passion and anointing, that it seemed the atmosphere became charged with supernatural faith from the Lord.

The following day the community assessed the damage from several tornados that had touched down that day, including an F-4 that struck certain parts of the city. I later learned that the F-4 storm was spinning in the direction of the homes of four of my staff members and headed in the direction of the two metal office buildings of the Voice of Evangelism. Eye witnesses said the storm split and moved in different directions about two miles from our offices. Other than a partially broken awning, there was no other damage. I believe it was the prayer of 225 people, speaking to and rebuking the storm, which moved the hand of the Lord to split the storm. For that we are very grateful.

Remember that spiritual principles are superior to natural laws and can trump the set laws of nature. Christ set new laws when He taught that we should give in order to receive, pray for our enemies instead of cursing them, turn the other cheek and not retaliate, and love your enemies as yourself (Matt. 5:38-44). While these instructions are the opposite of human nature, they reveal that obedience to the spiritual laws are the real source of favor and blessing from the Lord, and that God who created all laws can alter them on behalf of His followers.

Once believers understand this principle, it will be impossible to struggle with tithing and giving. They will understand that this spiritual seed grows to produce a spiritual harvest.

CHAPTER 5

The Significance of the Giving Life

SOMETIMES I AM asked why it is necessary to tithe and give. Giving is necessary, first of all, to keep the gospel moving forward. It costs money to operate ministries and churches, since it is rare to find people who will work and provide goods and services for nothing. Churches and ministries have to pay employees, utility bills, and mortgages, while at the same time provide for missions, the needy and so on.

There are benefits to the giver as well for their obedience and generosity. For example, it keeps your faith in action. Being a giver keeps you from becoming greedy. Giving keeps the promises of God activated and releases Kingdom blessings in your life. A giver will live under an open heaven. Giving is one way that God rewards you in heaven.

God's dwelling place in heaven is a city that contains books and recordings of activities that occur on earth. Part of the record keeping system is linked with the financial tithing and giving of the righteous on earth. In Malachi 3:16, there is a book of remembrance which records the names of those who fear God, witness to others of His name, and give tithe and offerings (see Malachi 3:16).

In Acts 10:1-4, the Italian centurion name Cornelius always prayed and gave money to the poor (called giving alms in the King James Version). An angel appeared and informed Cornelius that his prayers and giving had come up before God as a memorial (Acts 10:4). Notice that both his prayers and giving of alms gained the attention of God in His heavenly Temple.

This concept is further explained in Hebrew 7:8 when the writer speaks of how tithe was received by the priest at the Temple in Jerusalem. It is written, "Here mortal men receive tithes, but there he receives them, of whom it is witnessed that he lives" (Heb. 7:8). Thus, our giving on earth is recognized in heaven.

In the Bible, the word tithe in Hebrew is *ma'aser*, meaning *tenth*. The idea actually originated in ancient Mesopotamia with the concept that God gave you ten fingers with which to work, so you should bring one tenth of the grain, fruit or livestock to the temple and present it in appreciation, as well as for the provision of the priesthood of that particular temple. Thus tithe is linked to the blessing that comes through the works of your hands.

When the Apostle Paul was conducting missionary journeys, he depended upon the financial gifts of churches to provide for ship travel, food, support of poor churches, and other ministry needs. One church at Philippi consistently gave offerings for Paul's travel expenses and the needs of other churches. When thanking these believers, he wrote that it was "not that I desire a gift but that fruit may abound to your account" (Phil 4:17). Another translation reads, "Not that I seek or am eager for [your] gift, but I do seek and am eager for the fruit which increases to your credit [the harvest of blessing that is accumulating to your account] (AMP).

The good deeds and financial gifts that we give on earth are observed in heaven and even build a memorial there (Acts 10:1-4). These actions are accredited to our account. When this church financed Paul's journey to preach the gospel and win souls, those souls who converted to Christ were added to the believer's account in heaven. The blessings for a giver are both heavenly and earthly, as indicated in Mark 10:29-30:

> "Verily I say unto you, There is no man that hath left house, or brethren, or sisters, or father, or mother, or wife, or children, or lands, for my sake, and the gospel's, But he shall receive an hundredfold now in this

time, houses, and brethren, and sisters, and mothers, and children, and lands, with persecutions; and in the world to come eternal life."

In Philippians 4:19 Paul reveals, "But my God shall supply all your need according to His riches in glory by Christ Jesus" (Phil. 4:19). According to Greek scholar Rick Renner, the word *supply* means *cram a net, to level up something, and to provide for what is missing*. The original word referred to "on behalf of the choir."

The imagery is that the large choirs practiced in theatres for months and eventually the time came to travel and perform. However, after months of hard work the choir fund had run dry. Now their dreams were shattered and their work seemed in vain. A rich man heard of their plight and contributed a large donation on behalf of the choir. The idea is that, after you have been obedient to God and it appears you are going to run low or run out, the Spirit of the Lord will step in and contribute to your support.

God will contribute to assist you in your time of need. The word *need* is a Greek word meaning, "a necessity, business and employment." We could say that God will supply all of your employment necessities! The Lord supplies this according to His riches. The Greek word for riches here is *ploutos*, which refers to wealth, money, bestowment and abundance. Imagine the riches and abundance God has, including owning the cattle on a thousand hills (Ps. 50:10).

There is, however, a difference between God supplying your need according to your need and your need according to His riches. I heard my friend Walter Hallam explain this by saying that, if a stranger came to you needing money for gas and he was sincere, you would give him ten dollars to meet the need. However, if your wife came to you needing money for gas, you might just give her a couple of fifty dollar bills. You provide for your wife, not just for the need, but from your personal supply of riches. Why? Because you know your wife and have a relationship with her.

DON'T ASK ONLY THAT THE NEED BE MET

When I heard this, I realized that too often believers seek the Lord in their times of need and ask only for the need to be met: "God I need a job as soon as possible...I need a breakthrough in my finances...I need money to pay a house payment and a car payment now...this bill is coming due and I need help to pay it..."

If we only pray for the need to be met, then we will only expect for the need to be met, when God may desire a greater increase for you, but you are not believing or expecting it to occur. As an example, Peter had fished all night and caught nothing. Christ asked to borrow Peter's boat to stand in while preaching to a multitude on the shoreline. After the sermon, Christ told Peter to take *nets* and go fishing for a great catch of fish (Luke 5:1-7). Peter obeyed but only dragged *a net* (one net) through the water. The catch of fish was so overwhelming that Peter called other boats to participate in this fish harvest! The Lord not only met the need of Peter to fill his net, but this overflow blessing required nets to contain the fish.

Christ borrowed five loaves and two fishes to feed five thousand and performed a miracle of multiplication to meet the need of feeding the crowd. However, more than the need was supplied when twelve baskets of fish and bread were left over (Mark 8:19). To meet a need is *just enough;* but to receive according to *God's riches in glory* is to supply beyond the need and meet the need with some left over.

Perhaps a more detailed manner of prayer is to pray, "Lord, according to your abundant riches, release to me your abundant supply..." Or "Lord, according to your riches in glory, provide above and beyond what is needed..." Often individuals will seek things, instead of seeking the source of blessings. Christ made this clear in Matthew 6:31-33:

> *"Therefore take no thought, saying, What shall we eat? or, What shall we drink? or, Wherewithal shall we be clothed? (For after all these things do the Gentiles seek:) for your heavenly Father knoweth ye have need of all these things. But seek ye first the kingdom of God, and his righteousness; and all these things shall be added unto you."*

EXPECT A SUPERNATURAL BREAKTHROUGH

Without faith it is impossible to please God, and those seeking Him in faith will be rewarded by Him for their faith (Heb. 11:6). When the paraplegic man at the golden gate heard Peter say, "Look on us," he paid attention and expected to receive from them (Acts 3:5). Expectancy is the seed that helps the impossible to be made possible. Expectancy is the emotion that is triggered when faith is sensed in the human spirit. It is the motivation that causes a blind man to cry out to Christ for healing (Luke 18:38-42), and a woman suffering twelve years with a hemorrhage to sneak into a crowd and touch the hem of Jesus's garment to be cured (Matt. 9:20-22).

Christ spoke a parable, recorded in Luke 18, and concluded it with these words, "Nevertheless, when the Son of Man comes, will He really find faith on the earth?" (Luke 18:8). The cares of life, deceitfulness of riches, and lust of things will choke the Word of God in your heart (Matt. 13:22) and stop your fruitfulness or your productivity. After prayer and following the basic instructions above, then live in a realm of continual expectancy that your Heavenly Father knows your needs even before you ask (Matt. 6:8), and has compassion on you in your time of need.

THE ALEXANDER KERR STORY

Alexander Kerr was converted to Christ at age fourteen under the ministry of D. L. Moody. Following his conversion, Kerr joined the Presbyterian Church. In 1902 Kerr read a book called, "Judah's Scepter and Joseph's Birthright," a writing that revealed Jacob's vow to give God the tithe. In the story, Jacob returned home twenty years later with so much wealth that he attempted to give a portion of it away to his brother Esau.

On June 1, 1902 Kerr made a vow to God to set aside a percentage of his income for the work of God. He immediately began giving his tithe. At the time he held a mortgage on a home, owed numerous bills, and was burdened with many personal cares.

After three months, blessings began to occur. That same year he started a company called the Kerr Jar Factory. The jars were manufactured in the city of San Francisco at his new factory, and God's blessing was poured out upon the business.

Then in 1906 an unexpected event occurred when the earthquake struck northern California in the San Francisco area. Kerr was out of state when the quake struck, and he received a wire stating that the entire city was devastated. Businessmen who were meeting with him at the time said, "Kerr, you are a ruined man." Kerr replied, "I don't believe it, or if I am, the Bible is not true. God will not go back on His promises."

Then Kerr received a second wire which read, "Your factory is in the heart of the fire. No doubt all is lost." It took many days to search through the city to receive information about the damage done in the quake. Then Kerr received this wire: "Everything for a mile and a half on all sides of the factory burned; but your factory was miraculously saved."

The factory was a two story wooden building with huge tanks where glass was melted. There was also oil that was used for fuel so this would have been flammable. The fire raged on all sides, creeping up to the wooden fence surrounding the building and even scorching it. The flames leaped outside on all sides, but not a single jar was cracked.

This miracle so impacted Kerr that in 1912, he began placing in each of his jars a small leaflet called, "God's Cure for Poverty," which encouraged people to tithe and give to the work of God. Today Ruth Kerr, a Baptist believer, runs the company out of Los Angeles and the organization still tithes today.

MAKE FRIENDS OF MAMMON

It is said that the Bible contains about five hundred verses on prayer and another five hundred on faith. However, there are about eight hundred that deal with money or stewardship. In the New Testament are two passages that seem to contradict each other, one in Matthew and one in Luke:

> *"No man can serve two masters: for either he will hate the one, and love the other; or else he will hold to the one, and despise the other. Ye cannot serve God and mammon."*
>
> –MATTHEW 6:24

"And I say unto you, Make to yourselves friends of the mammon of unrighteousness; that, when ye fail, they may receive you into everlasting habitations.

"He that is faithful in that which is least is faithful also in much: and he that is unjust in the least is unjust also in much.

"If therefore ye have not been faithful in the unrighteous mammon, who will commit to your trust the true riches?

"And if ye have not been faithful in that which is another man's, who shall give you that which is your own?"

– LUKE 16:9-12

Matthew records Christ telling us to make no friends of mammon, while the Luke reference indicates that Christ's instruction is to make friends of mammon. The first question is, what is mammon? The word comes from the Aramaic, *mam* and *nos*, meaning prosperity.

Those speaking Syriac Aramaic believed that mammon was the god of riches and wealth. According to some scholars, the word is akin to the Hebrew word for being steadfast and firm. A well-known Hebrew word a-men or *amen* is a word we say that means, "So be it;" but amen is also a word used to indicate that the word spoken can be trusted. The Gesenius Lexicon points out that the word mammon is derived from the word for treasure. For example, in Genesis 43:23, the word treasure is *matmown,* which is similar to the word mammon.

In the setting of Luke 16, verses 1-8 teach of a steward who is overseeing his master's finances, and the emphasis is on not wasting the master's money. In verses 19-31 is the story of a rich man who did not care for a sick, poor man who was begging at the gates of his home. That entire chapter covers the subject of making right decisions with your possessions and finances. It is between these two stories that Christ inserted the statement, "make friends of mammon." Thus the apparent contradiction is that on one hand, you cannot serve God and mammon, and on the other hand, you are to make friends of mammon.

To glean further insight from this statement, look at various translations of verse 9:

"I tell you, use worldly wealth to gain friends for yourselves, so that when it is gone, you will be welcomed into eternal dwellings." (NIV)

"And I say to you, make friends for yourselves by means of the wealth of unrighteousness, so that when it fails, they will receive you into the eternal dwellings." (NASB)

"And I tell you, make friends for yourselves by means of unrighteous mammon (deceitful riches, money, possessions), so that when it fails, they [those you have favored] may receive and welcome you into the everlasting habitations (dwellings)." (AMP)

"I tell you, use your worldly resources to benefit others and make friends. In this way, your generosity stores up a reward for you in heaven." (NLT)

The message seems to be, use your resources to make friends among those who are unsaved and help them when possible. You may eventually win them to Christ and you will be welcomed and rewarded in eternity. This is the true meaning of laying up for yourselves treasure in heaven (Matt. 6:19-21).

Several years ago, one of my pastor friends became involved in a parade that had absolutely nothing spiritual connected with it and was full of unsaved people. Later the pastor was challenged in the city court over an issue, and one of the biggest Christian fighters in the city sent his own lawyer to defend the pastor and his church, just because he liked the fact that they had treated the sinners well.

Many years ago I was ministering in a small community. Unknown to me, a young man attended the meeting whose father was involved with the crime syndicate in a major city. That night the young man was converted and told his father. After the service I received a call in a restaurant from a man who was threatening me with harm. I called the police, and they showed up and recommended that I leave where I was staying and change locations.

As I walked out of the restaurant, three men were in a car and I recognized one as the son of a very godly woman in the local church. I also knew he was one of the drug kingpins in the county and his mother was praying for his conversion. The fellow said, "Stone, come over here. I just heard on the police scanner that you had a threat. Don't worry." He pulled out a 357 from under his seat and said, "If anybody messes with you, they'll have to come through us first!"

Never have I been so thankful to have sinner friends! Remember, it was Jesus who was called a "friend of sinners" (Matt. 11:19), so I was in good company.

USING THE WORLD SYSTEM

Another statement was made in Luke, in reference to being a good steward and being faithful in little: "*The children of this world are in their generation wiser than the children of light*" (Luke 16:8). How is the world wiser that the children of God?

Consider many of the inventions over the past one hundred years. In the 1920s, what if Christian businessmen had seized the opportunity to become involved in the first major radio station? What if the same had occurred with the invention of television, satellite or Internet?

In the earlier days of the Full Gospel movement, television was considered an evil tool among some and the Internet was thought to be the future mark of the beast system. Thus, at first these forms of technology were avoided because they were thought to be evil. In reality, both have served as the most powerful tools in world history to take the gospel to the nations. Had strong believers gotten their foot in the door with these early inventions, the world would be spending millions to use these resources, and believers would have an abundance of income to use for the needs of global ministry.

Scriptures are often used to indicate the danger of mixing the spiritual with the mundane and the world's system of operation.

> "*Love not the world neither the things that are in the world...*"
>
> – 1 JOHN 2:15

> "*The love of money is the root of all evil...*"
>
> – 1 TIM. 6:10

> "*The rich fall into temptation and a snare, and into many foolish and hurtful lusts.*"
>
> – 1 TIM 6:9

"Rich men, weep and howl for the miseries that shall come upon you..."

– JAMES 5:1

"I am rich and increased with goods and have need of nothing..."

– REV. 3:17

These Scriptures imply that being poor is better than being rich, and that if you are rich, you have too many challenges to deal with. However, the root of these warnings deals with trusting in riches and defining the real treasure of your heart. First Timothy 6:17-19 helps sum up the teaching:

"Charge them that are rich in this world, that they be not highminded, nor trust in uncertain riches, but in the living God, who giveth us richly all things to enjoy; That they do good, that they be rich in good works, ready to distribute, willing to communicate; Laying up in store for themselves a good foundation against the time to come, that they may lay hold on eternal life."

Jesus did not own earthly goods, which was mentioned earlier in this book. However, He was called a glutton and a winebibber for hanging out and eating with sinners, and He was called a friend of publicans and sinners (Matt. 11:19). Christ willingly forgave a woman caught in the act of adultery, even though she could have been stoned to death. He passed through Samaria, a city despised by the religious Jews, and ministered to the city prostitute, better known as the woman at the well.

Jesus had friends of mammon who supported His ministry. Luke records:

"And certain women, which had been healed of evil spirits and infirmities, Mary called Magdalene, out of whom went seven devils,

"And Joanna the wife of Chuza Herod's steward, and Susanna, and many others, which ministered unto Him of their substance."

– LUKE 8:2-3

Other translations say:

"Provided for him and them out of their personal belongings." (AMP)

"Contributing to their support out of their private means." (NASB)

"Contributing of their own resources to support Jesus and His disciples." (NLT)

The man who was Herod's steward was an overseer of a province with direct access to Herod's palace. Joanna was his wife and a supporter of Christ's ministry. Today, there are times when a woman will support a church or ministry, but the husband never attends church and might even try to hinder her from being a financial giver. In Christ's death, two secret disciples who were wealthy businessmen and friends of Christ—Nicodemus and Joseph of Arimathea—took charge of His body and placed it in Joseph's tomb. Christ made friends, and when He died, these friends received His body.

MAKING FRIENDS WITH PEOPLE IN THE WORLD SYSTEM

We are part of the world system. We go to school and college in the world system, and we work with people who are unrighteous and unbelievers. This cannot be avoided. We must work the system without allowing the system to corrupt us. We are in this world, but we are not of this world. It is both possible and necessary that we work with wolves without joining the pack.

The Bible gives us two excellent examples—Joseph and Daniel. Joseph lived and worked in the world system and in seventeen years, he was promoted from prison to second in charge. He started out as a servant and used his gift of interpreting dreams, which exalted him from a prisoner to second in charge over the treasure houses of Pharaoh. Joseph was given an Egyptian name, Zaphnath-Paaneah (Gen. 41:45), but his Hebrew name is always used in the biblical narrative.

Daniel was in the world system after being brought into Babylon as a Jewish captive at age seventeen. He and three of his companions seized the attention of the king, and all were trained as leader's in the king's court. Daniel remained there from age seventeen to age ninety, and he served in a high position while in Babylon.

After Daniel and his companions were chosen to be trained, the chief official renamed them. Their original names honored the God of Israel, but their new names were chosen to honor the false gods of Babylon. Daniel was renamed Belteshazzar, which honors the idol named Bel. Hananiah was renamed Shadrach and Mishel was renamed Meshach, both in honor of the idol god Akku. Azariah was given the name Abednego, which means servant of Nebo.

A key point is that Daniel, even though he was renamed Belteshazzar, never compromised and never identified himself with the Babylonian system. Seven times in the book of Daniel, he identified himself as, "I Daniel."

Both Joseph and Daniel were righteous and God-fearing men who worked closely with people and leaders in idolatrous nations. Yet they were able to influence those around them with their faith and with the supernatural abilities of their God. We might say that they worked in the world, but did not become corrupted by the world (John 17:17-18).

Christians—especially those who came from a traditional holiness background as I did—sometimes have a fear of becoming involved in the world or befriending people in the world for three reasons. The first fear is that being around a sinner might cause a believer to return to a lifestyle of sin. The second reason is that, being around the world and sinners might corrupt the faith of a believer. Lastly, being around things of the world could cause a believer to desire the things of the world, including a life of financial prosperity.

These things can happen and have indeed happened to some. But why should Christians have that fear? Is it because they do not have a strong enough relationship with Christ to keep from being drawn back into the world? Is it because they are passive, rather than bold, like Daniel? Notice that Daniel did not eat the king's meat or drink his wine, because he was determined not to defile himself. He continued to pray facing Jerusalem, despite a law forbidding prayer (Daniel 6). Joseph never worshipped any idol in Egypt, but maintained his faith in the God of Abraham. Both proved that it is possible to rise to the highest ranks of government influence and never compromise your convictions. Their uncompromising faith raised them from obscurity to leadership in two of the world's prophetic empires.

The trouble with some Christians today is that they have lost their influence among sinners. They are influenced by sinners rather than being the salt and light and influencing the world. Most sinners know hypocrites, but few know light-bearing saints who are able to preserve the things of God as they live and work among sinners. Christians should be living so that sinners are attracted to them.

Thankfully, believers are beginning to have an influence in the world arena. People are paying attention to Christians. Look at the worldwide success of the movie, The Passion of the Christ. This movie impacted both Christian and secular communities around the globe, and it stunned the Hollywood elite who never believed such a film could attract an audience. It grossed over six hundred million dollars, making it one of the most successful films of all times. Thanks to this movie, more Christian-themed films are now being produced and shown in theaters.

Look at the success of gospel music and Christian books. Secular publishers are now signing Christian authors, and secular record producers want to sign Christian musicians. Cable networks and satellites now carry Christian channels, allowing the gospel to go into any part of the world that has access to television or Internet.

When making friends of mammon, it is possible to use the secular world to promote the gospel and Christian themes. One of my pastor friends has thousands of members in his church, and he is noted for using movie themes and incorporating them into his messages. By doing this, he is effectively reaching a younger generation. Another pastor uses theatrical-type productions, often with actors who represent famous singers, and he reaches thousands. I have heard of people using Christian wrestlers, musicians, sports, and other such methods as the bait to bring in the lost, so they can be presented with a life-changing message that will influence them to serve Christ.

The Bible clearly teaches that we are not to put our trust and faith in money, or in any system that hands us money. Instead, we are taught to be a good steward and use money wisely to advance the Kingdom of God, win people to faith in Christ, and thereby have them as friends forever—in this life and in the life to come.

CHAPTER 6

Provision for All Blessings is Found in the Atonement

"For you know the grace of our Lord Jesus Christ, that
though He was rich, yet for your sakes He became poor,
that you through His poverty might become rich."

– 2 Corinthians 8:9 (NKJV)

ONE OF THE most unique insights you will ever learn is that God is concerned about every area of your life and not just the spiritual aspect. Our spiritual, redemptive blessings are provided as a ladder to eternity and a ticket to heaven. However, we presently live on a planet filled with wickedness, and we need God's favor and intervention in the emotional, physical and provisional areas of our lives.

Through Christ's atoning work, all areas of life are secured, including eternal life (Jude 21). By definition, the *atonement* is the spiritual work that was accomplished for us through the sufferings of Christ. By His atonement He bought pardon for our sins and reconciled mankind back to God (Col. 1:20). According to the Messianic prophecy recorded in Isaiah 53, Jesus Christ suffered to bring forth a threefold reconciliation that impacts the threefold nature of each human being—the body, soul and spirit (1 Thess. 5:23).

The first and highest level of the atonement brings redemption to our soul and spirit.

"He shall see of the travail of his soul, and shall be satisfied: by his knowledge shall my righteous servant justify many; for he shall bear their iniquities."

– ISAIAH 53:11

Our spirit is the eternal part of our three-part being, and our spirit needs to be born again by receiving Christ as Savior and Lord. Redemption through the blood that Christ shed on the cross is the church's greatest message for mankind. By redeeming us, Christ has bought us from the slave market of sin, released us from bondage, adopted us as sons and daughters (Gal 4:5), and in the end will bring us into the heavenly kingdom. That is the message of the gospel!

Second, Christ's suffering brought healing to the physical bodies of those who acknowledge God as their healer:

"But he was wounded for our transgressions, he was bruised for our iniquities: the chastisement of our peace was upon him; and with his stripes we are healed."

– ISAIAH 53:5

Prior to His crucifixion, Christ was beaten on His back by a Roman soldier, creating blood covered stripes and deep wounds on His body. These stripes that Christ took on His back were for our physical healing. This is clear in 1 Peter 2:24 when Peter wrote, "… with his stripes ye were healed." Peter penned this verse many years after Christ's suffering and he spoke in the past tense, meaning that Christ already provided for our healing when He was scourged prior to the crucifixion (Mark 15:15).

A third area of Christ's atoning work is often overlooked, but is also revealed in the prophetic vision of Isaiah:

"Surely he hath borne our griefs, and carried our sorrows: yet we did esteem him stricken, smitten of God, and afflicted."

– ISAIAH 53:4

Grief and sorrow are emotional feelings we have when we encounter a tragic event, such as the death of a loved one. We feel sorrow after a death because we miss the person, and we experience a time of grief as the reality of the loss seizes our heart. Jesus, however, carried our grief and sorrow, meaning that we can place our emotional weakness on Him and He will help carry our burdens.

Most major denominations in North America accept one or two of the above works of Christ, while others acknowledge all three. However, there is a fourth level of blessing that, in my many years of ministry, I never knew about until it was explained to me by Dr. John Miller. That set me on a journey to research the insights and implications of our blessings in the atonement.

Years ago, Dr. Miller and I were preparing to tape the television series on the meal that heals. Dr. Miller indicated that most churches emphasize only one aspect of the atonement. They believe that Christ's sufferings were for one purpose only, and that is the forgiveness of sins. Forgiveness of sins is the foundation of Christianity, and the primary emphasis of any believer or church should be to preach a redemptive covenant through the cross of Jesus Christ.

The Full Gospel message however, acknowledges a two-fold atonement, consisting of redemption of the spirit (forgiveness of sins) and physical healing which was also provided by the beating Christ took on His back, prior to the crucifixion (Isa 53:5; 1 Pet. 2:24). Most Full Gospel (Pentecostal and Charismatic) churches acknowledge that Jesus has the power today to heal the sick through the prayer of faith and the call for elders to pray for the sick based on James 5:14.

Yet, few Christians understand the third dimension of atonement—that emotional healing is also provided through the sufferings of Christ! The same churches that will preach salvation on Sunday morning and anoint the sick with oil on Sunday night, often send their members to a professional counselor or a psychologist to handle their emotional problems.

I believe in Christian counseling when necessary, especially when somebody has dealt with long term and severe problems. Yet, we read where Christ carried *"oppression, rejection and grief"* in His own body (Isa. 53:3). In Isaiah chapter 53, we read that Christ carried our sins to release us from our own sins, bore sickness to bring healing, and carried the emotional pains caused by oppression, rejection and grief so through His new covenant we would be made whole or complete through Him (1 Thess. 5:23). Counseling may discover the root of the addictions and problems, but the power of Christ is needed for a complete deliverance from the addiction or the emotional bondage.

As we discussed the various dimensions of the atonement, I was taken aback when Doc said, "Did you know that all of our material blessing were also a part of Christ's atoning work?" That comment seized my attention. How could the sufferings of Christ and His death and resurrection be connected to our personal blessings, especially provision for our material needs?

When I have made this statement in the past, some Christians look at me as if I have fallen off a cliff. Some think it sounds heretical. I believe this is because they do not understand the full and complete work of Christ, and they have a secular and worldly view of prosperity and blessing. In their mind, blessing alludes only to earthly and material prosperity; or as they interpret it, "You mean Jesus died so I could have a nice house and a better car?"

That is *not* the intended meaning of the Lord providing an avenue of provision as part of the atonement. I have made it clear for years that man's definition of blessing, provision, and even prosperity is not the same definition that the Lord gives.

Only when believers understand both the atonement and the Biblical meaning of true success and prosperity can they understand this concept: Christ's atonement covers all of our needs in life, including our personal needs. To understand the assignment of Christ, we must first look back to the law that Christ lived under before He sealed a New Covenant at His death and resurrection.

JESUS AND THE TORAH

When God established His covenant with Abraham, He promised him a seed (a son), a nation, and a land (Gen. 17:4-6). Generations later, Moses brought forth that very seed of Abraham into their Promised Land that is now called Israel. In order to preserve divine order in the Hebrew nation, God revealed His commandments and principles to

Moses on Mount Sinai (Exod. chapters 19-31), giving Moses a set of divine instructions that Israel was commanded to follow.

God motivated the nation by initiating the blessings and curses that are found in Deuteronomy chapter 28. If the Hebrew people were obedient to God's moral, ceremonial and judicial instructions, they would experience blessings in every area of their lives. Their land would produce food and their trees would produce fruit, their businesses would prosper, and their family and animals would be healthy (Deut. 28:1-14).

On the other hand, if the people chose to disobey God, they would encounter the disfavor of God and experience curses. The disfavor of God would also permit negative circumstances to arise in their land.

Part of the curse included terror in the land, drought, disease, feeble livestock, famine and lack (Deut. 28:14-45). The purpose of these blessings and curses was to motivate the Hebrew nation to completely follow the Lord, and not to follow the idolatry and sins of the surrounding pagan nations. Also, the future Messiah would need a pure linage from a holy nation, and the Hebrews were chosen for this purpose. Therefore, they were prohibited from intermarrying with pagan tribes that would corrupt and pervert the lineage of Christ.

There were so many restrictions and commandments that even the New Testament writers noted the difficulty for one person to keep all of the law. Yet, if one part of the law was disobeyed, it was as though all of the law was broken (see Romans 7 and 8). However, from Moses to the time of Christ, there was one man who was completely obedient to the commandments of God in every area of His life, throughout His entire life. He is the only person who can be called sinless, meaning that He had no sin the entire time that He lived on earth. That man was Jesus Christ (2 Cor. 5:21).

Christ walked morally upright, never breaking the moral law (1 Pet. 2:22). He fulfilled the picture of the Mosaic sacrifices—the lamb at Passover (Exod. 12), the brass serpent on the pole (Num. 21:8-9), and the red heifer sacrifice (Num. 19)—thus fulfilling the sacrificial expectations in the Torah. He bore our sins on the cross, thus satisfying the judicial requirements of a sin offering (Heb. 10:8-18).

To lay claim to all of the wonderful benefits and blessings found in the instructions of the Torah would require that a person, group of people, or the entire nation obey every commandment and statute written therein. Biblical history reveals that most individuals, tribes, and the nation of Israel continually failed in this regard.

However, look at Christ. Since He "knew no sin" (1 Pet. 2:22), Jesus was the only sinless man who could legally lay claim to every *blessing* promised by God to a person willing to live a covenant life and obey every command. Jesus was qualified to lay claim to *every promise*, which included every promise for physical blessing, spiritual increase, and financial prosperity that is guaranteed in Deuteronomy 28. Remember, Christ never broke the written instructions of God. He only broke the traditions of men (Mark 7:1-13).

One part of the blessing was prosperity for those who would keep the commandments of God:

> *"Keep therefore the words of this covenant, and do them, that ye may prosper in all that ye do."*
>
> – DEUT. 29:9

> *"And you shall remember the LORD your God, for it is He who gives you power to get wealth, that He may establish His covenant which He swore to your fathers, as it is this day."*
>
> – DEUT. 8:18 (NKJV)

This prosperity promise was connected to the entire land of Israel. God would bless Israel with vines and fruit bearing trees, their animals would be healthy, and their wives would birth strong children.

Christ had none of the above. He purchased no property for himself, and He pruned no natural vineyards at His own private estate. He invested no income in animals or livestock, and His financial portfolio was nonexistent. Jesus remained unmarried and, of course, He never fathered children. He was not married to Mary Magdalene as some heretics have suggested, but His true bride would be comprised of individual believers from every nation—His called out ones. His Word—that is, the seed of the Word, according to Matthew 13:18-30—would conceive millions of sons and daughters into the heavenly kingdom.

He was born in a stable and placed in a borrowed manger. He preached from borrowed boats, stayed in the homes of close friends, and ate from the tables of disciples who invited Him for dinner. He rode into Jerusalem on a donkey that was loaned to Him, and borrowed a rich man's tomb to be buried in for three days.

Christ fulfilled every moral, sacrificial and judicial command; yet He refused to accept the prosperity blessings promised to those who would obey God's instructions (Josh. 1:7; 1 Kings 2:3; 1 Chron. 22:13; 2 Chron. 20:20; Neh. 2:20; Ps. 122:6). Why? Let's look at the possible reasons.

First, Jesus was not connected to earthly things, because His kingdom was spiritual and heavenly in nature (John 8:23; 18:36). His home was with His heavenly Father, and He chose to have no ties to things, possessions and earthly goods. He knew that His human life would be for a short season, and then He would return to His Father in heaven (John 14:1-2).

Imagine this. What would Christ have done with bags of money, land, houses and possessions? Can you imagine the arguments over who should split His wealth when He ascended to heaven? The disciples were often so carnal that they might have gone to court and divided the possessions among themselves instead of traveling the world, spreading the gospel, and most dying as martyrs. Just as some today, they might have been so caught up in building a museum or a monument to particular events, that the gospel could have been hindered.

Had He owned anything, those things would have become a holy relic, a spiritual monument, or a point of debate between the churches. Today in the Holy Land the Catholics, Greek Orthodox, Russian Orthodox and others draw lines in buildings to mark the "real spot" where Christ ministered. As an example, there is a physical division in the Church of the Nativity in Bethlehem among three groups. The Vatican has a piece of His cross, a shroud exists that is believed to prove the resurrection, and even the skulls of Peter and Paul are found in three different locations in Rome. Imagine the confusion if Christ had initiated and left an earthly kingdom of possessions when He departed earth!

I believe that another reason Christ rejected the prosperity blessings promised in the law can be found in a powerful passage in 2 Corinthians 8:9:

"For ye know the grace of our Lord Jesus Christ, that, though he was rich, yet for your sakes he became poor, that ye through his poverty might be rich".

I seldom quote from other translations, but notice how this passage is translated in the Amplified version:

"For you are becoming progressively acquainted with and recognizing more strongly and clearly the grace of our Lord Jesus Christ (His kindness, His gracious generosity, His undeserved favor and spiritual blessing), [in] that though He was [so very] rich, yet for your sakes He became [so very] poor, in order that by His poverty you might become enriched (abundantly supplied)."

Here is the verse in the New Living Translation:

"You know how full of love and kindness our Lord Jesus Christ was. Though he was very rich, yet for your sakes he became poor, so that by his poverty he could make you rich."

Christ could have chosen a road of great material prosperity. According to Luke, he had numerous wealthy individuals who supported his ministry:

"And certain women, which had been healed of evil spirits and infirmities, Mary called Magdalene, out of whom went seven devils, And Joanna the wife of Chuza Herod's steward, and Susanna, and many others, which ministered unto him of their substance."

– LUKE 8:2-3

I once heard Dr. E.L. Terry explain from his research who he believed Joanna and Susanna were. He said that Susanna might have been the wife of Joseph of Arimathea, a wealthy tin trader who owned many ships and was a secret disciple of Christ (John 3:1-12; Matt.

27:57,60). The husband of Joanna was Herod's steward, who would have assisted in Herod's building programs. Historically, Herod was a great builder who spent years enlarging Jerusalem. Joanna's husband would have been involved in this and would likely have been financially sound. These wealthy wives were linked to Christ's ministry and supported Him financially.

If Jesus had been motivated by His flesh, He could have purchased a summer home in the mountains of Galilee, a special getaway in the Judean wilderness, or a winter cabin on Mount Hermon. Using His popularity and tapping into His "partner base," Christ could have invested in vineyards in the Jezreel Valley, or organized a fishing business by partnering with Peter and John. Instead Christ ascended to heaven, leaving no possessions on earth—just zealous disciples who would shake the world and create a holy nation (1 Pet. 2:9), known as the church!

Christ rejected the prosperity aspect of the covenant and instead released blessings to us if we would walk in His Word. He became poor so that we could become rich. Some suggest that the word *rich* in 2 Corinthians 8:9 refers only to spiritual riches. They point out that the word rich is used when speaking of rich in mercy (Eph. 2:4), rich in faith (James 2:5), and rich in good works (1 Tim. 6:18). But a word study reveals the true meaning.

The Greek word for the verb *rich* in 2 Corinthians 8:9 is a common Greek word, *plouteo,* and refers to being increased with goods and having acquired wealth. The same Greek word is used in the New Testament when indicating that people have financial and material wealth (Rev. 18:3; 15:19). It is used to indicate a wealthy person (Matt. 19:23), including Joseph of Arimathea, who is called a rich man in Matthew 27:57.

If a theologian assumes that this promise of Christ becoming poor that we might be rich refers only to spiritual riches, then we must ask, when Christ became poor to make us rich, then what was His poverty? Christ had the gifts of mercy, good works, and great faith, and was rich in these; He was not poor in these gifts. Being poor in the context of the verse refers to natural and earthly poverty, not spiritual poverty.

Since a workman is worthy of his hire (Luke 10:7), and a Christian leader is worthy of double honor (1 Tim. 5:17), if anyone deserved riches because of his ministry it was Christ, who healed all that were oppressed of the devil (Acts 10:38). Christ, however, willfully forfeited the prosperity and natural blessings promised for obedience to the law, and instead passed these blessings on to His righteous and obedient spiritual family. He knew that His followers would need these blessings in their daily lives. God wants His children to enjoy abundant life (John 10:10) and serve as an example to the unsaved and the unbelieving scoffer of how good God is and how blessed we are to have a covenant with Him.

WHAT ABOUT THE POOR BELIEVERS OVERSEAS?

The above information immediately brings up a common question from those opposed to the idea of blessing. The question stems from this comment: "Material blessing only works in America or a modern and wealthy nation. This does not work in third world countries."

First, ask yourself why these material and financial blessings are found in America and other modern nations. Historically, it was England under King James that had the Bible translated into the English language and printed for the general population in 1611. From that moment on, blessings and wealth poured into the British nation as, at one time, the "sun never set on the British empire."

America's three main founding documents that created our nation—the Declaration of Independence, the Bill of Rights and the Constitution—are all based upon the Torah (five books of Moses), the prophets, and the Gospels. Our spiritual and material blessings are released from God as the nation was founded on Biblical, Judeo-Christian principles, and our laws were centered upon the Law of God.

If we look today at nations reeling in poverty—India, for example—we find a nation of people who worship and pray to thousands of false gods and idols. These idols are powerless to bring provision. God blesses His Word and those who worship Him. America has been blessed, I believe, because in the past we have followed God's Word.

Multitudes of Christians living in foreign countries, however, are living in extreme poverty or surrounded by poverty. Some people who are critical of any form of prosperity teaching often say, "Prosperity doesn't work overseas. If it did, the poor people in these nations would be living in big homes and driving new cars." Once again, this is someone's *personal concept* of prosperity—a big home and a new car. The meaning of Biblical prosperity goes far beyond the Western mindset.

Every nation has a perception of what it means to be blessed or prosperous. For example, in America, if a single college student lives in a nice apartment and can afford the monthly payment he or she is blessed. If a single mom and her two children live in a fully furnished home and she is making the mortgage payments on time, this is a great blessing. Any person, anywhere in the world, who has food, shelter and clothing is blessed, as Christ taught that these three things are the basic needs in a person's life (Matt. 6:25-31).

The Western perception of prosperity is a hindrance in understanding true prosperity. If a person is driving a new BMW someone will comment that they must be rich. Yet, one of the wealthiest men in America dressed in overalls and drove a thirty-year-old pickup truck. Most multi-millionaires drive cars that are at least six years old. Seeing a man in denim overalls driving an old pickup truck would cause some to suggest that the fellow is poor and doesn't have much money. Yet in reality, this man owned hundreds of major stores across America.

Prosperity to some is based upon a perception of the *value of the things* we own, and this is exactly the opposite of what Christ taught:

> *"And He said to them, "Take heed and beware of covetousness, for one's life does not consist in the abundance of the things he possesses."*
> – Luke 12:15 (NKJV)

When considering Christians in a poverty stricken nation, the poverty is not the fault of the Christians, but is often linked to areas bound by dictators and criminals, as well as the worship of false gods. In many countries, the entire nation follows a false god or gods and their beliefs are filled with the occult and superstition, which opens the door to poverty, evil spirits and physical sickness.

Having been to Africa several times, I observed the financial corruption among the government leaders. One ministry sent two million dollars to Africa to build a hospital, and a government leader in the nation stole the money and bought a personal business. He paid off lawyers to prevent the ministry from suing him. This happened twice in the same country!

Goods and money sent for the poor are often stolen by corrupt government officials, or by people working at the ports, airports and banks. We once sent a large generator to Haiti and the church never received it because it was stolen by a government official and was never recovered. At times huge shipments of food never make to the needy. This is why you should know the people on the ground in these areas before supporting them.

God's Word even says that He cannot bless and prosper any nation that is corrupt, or worships idols, or bows before gods of wood, hay and stone. It is the adversary, not God, who motivates corrupt and evil men to pad their pockets while their own people suffer. In the time of Saul, the first king of Israel became spiritually rebellious and his unwise decisions caused the people in his kingdom to be in debt, distressed and discontented (1 Sam. 22:2).

Biblical prosperity, or having an abundance to see your needs met, is not a blank check for anyone who wants to cash it. It is a heavenly promise that is tapped into by the righteous who follow God's Word in life and conduct. When people live in this manner, they are blessed according to His (Christ's) riches in glory (Philippians 4:19).

Missionaries often report how God blesses these poorer nations on their *own level of blessing*. When we stop comparing our price, quality, and name brand belongings with the rest of the world and understand how God meets the true needs of His people, we begin to see that God's blessings for believers are global and not limited to North America or the west. For example, a missionary in India does not need a car that will use gas. He needs a bicycle. In Vietnam if a pastor has a small motorbike, this transportation is better and more practical than a car or a truck that would be more useful in America. In South America a horse or a mule is far more valuable that a pickup truck, since mules can climb mountains that trucks can't climb. Can you imagine an American CEO riding a rickshaw to work each morning or tying a mule or a camel to a parking space outside the office all day?

The same can be said about food and clothes. In America, we will take friends out to a nice restaurant for dinner. In the third world countries they consider themselves blessed to have rice every day. They don't require more and do not ask for more than what they need. In America, we consider clothes important because in the business realm, we are judged by our appearance. In many foreign nations, receiving a shipment of nice used clothing from America is like a free shopping trip to the mall.

Does God prosper and bless those believers who do not live in a Western nation? Certainly He does. Jesus said men would give to you (Luke 6:38). Prosperity covers physical, spiritual and material wealth. The poor believers may have fewer material possessions but are often rich in faith (James 2:5). This strong faith produces, for example, miraculous healings and testimonies of God's supernatural power to meet their physical needs without medical assistance.

In America we have experienced great material prosperity in recent decades. As we give away material blessings to our brothers and sisters in need, in return, they often can impart a level of faith and trust in God that we in the West are missing. We minister substance to them and they pray for us in return. Their material needs are met and we receive spiritual impartation. Having conducted mission evangelism in stadiums and outdoor events, I can testify that the love and simple faith from these believers is actually greater than material wealth, and it warms the heart like nothing else can.

THERE IS A WARNING

There is a warning for those who are prosperous with material goods. The Bible warns not to trust in uncertain riches (1 Tim. 6:17), and it warns against loving money (1 Tim. 6:10). We should understand that the more things you possess, the more cares of life you will encounter.

Anyone who invests in the stock market and commodities knows that riches can be uncertain, because profits are based upon cycles and world events. The wealthier you become the more cares of life you will encounter (Luke 21:34). Multiple homes must be cared for; you will require more insurance to protect your belongings, and alarm systems to prevent break-ins and robberies. Property needs constant repairs. It will cost money when you have money!

Someone I know is a close friend of one of America's billionaires. This man appears confident in public, but spends much time worrying about losses that come through his investments. With great material and financial prosperity comes great responsibility.

Paul understood the dangers of trusting in riches when he wrote:

> *"But those who desire to be rich fall into temptation and a snare, and into many foolish and harmful lusts which drown men in destruction and perdition. For the love of money is a root of all kinds of evil, for which some have strayed from the faith in their greediness, and pierced themselves through with many sorrows."*
>
> – 1 Tim. 6:9-10 (NKJV)

The only way that a person with extreme wealth can break the back of greed and fear of economic loss is to give away a portion of their earnings and profits to charitable organizations, churches, ministries of their choice, and those organizations that are making an impact in the lives of others. Releasing a portion of your income (called tithe and offering in the Scripture) is a sure way to be a blessing to others, as well as to prevent a spirit of greed from controlling your life.

Occasionally I speak to a gentleman who has been extremely successful during his lifetime, and one year brought in over fifty million dollars. He has even built schools and been a great help to the community and the state in which he lives. But through a series of unfortunate events, he lost much of what he had earned. I spoke to him recently and asked him about his future plans. He said, "You know, they can take my money and material goods because that stuff comes and goes; but they can't take my faith in God!" He then grinned and said, "I have a gift to make money. When all of this is settled and over, I will simply go back and do what I did when I had nothing to start with. I will start with my faith, and God will bless me again."

He did not say this in arrogance, he said this because deep inside he knows he has planted good seed that will eventually bring a harvest, and he knows that God helped him in the beginning and God will help him again.

Believers must operate in wisdom and keep selfishness and greed from their lives to ensure the continual favor of the Lord in their situation. Years ago I was invited to one of the most beautiful homes I had ever been in, and had lunch with a man who once had one of the fastest growing businesses in America, with tens of thousands of workers around the nation. At one time, his company stock was the doing so well that people were clamoring to ride the tide of prosperity.

This man, who was a shrewd and intelligent businessman, made several errors in judgment, thinking that these decisions were simply a wise move and no harm would be done. In reality, it was those decisions that eventually caused the stock to plummet and him to be removed as the CEO of the company. Many people's jobs and lives were affected by his decisions, including some of my own close ministry friends and partners.

The point is, the greater the blessing, the greater the responsibility and the more wisdom one needs to properly handle the wealth. I am convinced that in these last days, there will be a need for billions of dollars to complete the kingdom assignments of reaching people with the Gospel according to Matthew 24:14, and of caring for the poor around the world. This level of financial blessing must pass into the hands of those who are in covenant with God and who are already givers and will use their increase to benefit the kingdom. It will come into the hands of those whom God knows can be entrusted with such a measure of wealth.

THE ATONEMENT COVERS EVERY NEED

Each and every one of our spiritual blessings are found through Christ and the redemptive work He accomplished at the cross. Our healing was purchased as He took the stripes upon His back (Isa. 53:5; 1 Pet.

2:24). Our salvation was sealed by His death on the cross (Rom. 5:10-12). Our emotional well being was secured because He carried our oppression, grief, sorrow and rejection (Isa. 53:7-10). After receiving His redemptive plan for our lives, the blessings that follow are spiritual, physical, emotional and material as we succeed with the works of our hands and as we follow and continue to obey God's will. Christ refused to be rich in order that we may be rich—in grace, favor and blessings. This is why John wrote:

> "Beloved, I wish above all things that you might prosper and be in health, even as your soul prospers."

> — 3 JOHN 2

Notice that prosperity and health are conditional on your soul prospering. This agrees with the words of Christ that, if we seek first the kingdom of God and His righteousness, then all these things shall be added unto us (Matt. 6:33). The atoning work of Christ covers *all* the needs of the human family—the need for acceptance and forgiveness, the need for love and peace, the need for blessing and security, and the need for blessing and abundant life.

While many churches preach the salvation message and the healing promises of the Covenant, we must understand that Christ came to give us a more abundant life through Him. Your spiritual and natural prosperity is in the finished work of Christ! Remember that it is written, *"And my God shall supply all your need according to His riches in glory by Christ Jesus"* (Phil 4:19).

Anything that is necessary for an abundant life and for the fulfillment of His purposes, God will provide. And He will provide according to His *riches in glory*, if you will only ask and obey.

CHAPTER 7

Ways That the Lord Gives Provision

P ROVISION REPRESENTS NOT only that which you need to live, but also the resources necessary to successfully complete your God-ordained assignment. A carpenter requires tools, a builder needs supplies and so on. Even among God's own people, there are times when they challenge, not the ability, but the willingness of God to provide for the needs of His people. In the wilderness, the Israelites asked:

> "Behold, He struck the rock,
> So that the waters gushed out,
> And the streams overflowed.
> Can He give bread also?
> Can He provide meat for His people?"
>
> – Ps. 78:20 (NKJV)

The people had witnessed God's ability but were now questioning His willingness. The Hebrew word for provide is *kuwn*, and is a primitive root word meaning to erect or to stand perpendicular. The imagery is to set something upright and firm, and is figuratively used to lift someone up and cause them to prosper.

In Acts chapter 3 when Peter lifted up the man born lame, as the man was being physically picked up, his legs received strength and he stood on his own. This is the idea behind the word "provide" in Psalm 78:20. When the Lord reaches His hand toward you, He picks you up and you receive strength to stand, function properly, and prosper in your walk.

Often, believers have a mental image that they are required to do nothing except sit and wait for God to move on their behalf. However, faith must have a partner. God always works in co-operation with a person; not *without* a person. God sent ten plagues with His *hand*, but released them through the *mouth* of Moses. Moses spoke and God moved. This principle is important, as God is moved by your faith, and your faith requires action. Faith without works is dead (James 2:20).

With this in mind, there are several ways that God can open a road of provision for your life's journey.

1. GOD BLESSES THE WORKS OF YOUR HANDS

Some in our society expect to work as little as possible to get as much as possible in the shortest time possible. An entitlement mentality, known in the Ten Commandments as covetousness, says that I should let someone else work hard while I desire and demand a portion of their earnings. This way of thinking has even corrupted the minds of some believers who desire an easy solution or quick fix without any effort, and certainly without stretching their faith and patience.

I see this same "make it easy" approach among believers who want to get to heaven without living holy, or people who want to be a Christian without attending church, praying, reading the Bible or engaging in any scriptural disciplines. Folks want to get prayers answered but never repent of their own sins. People want to be blessed without sacrifice.

Nothing good comes to us that easily, and laziness or get-rich-quick schemes are not the way to earn a living. It takes hard work, effort and wisdom to succeed in life. God blesses the works of your hands—that is, the work you are paid to do each day. Deuteronomy 16:15 reads:

> *"Seven days shalt thou keep a solemn feast unto the LORD thy God in the place which the LORD shall choose: because the LORD thy God shall bless thee in all your increase, and in all the works of your hands, therefore thou shall surely rejoice."*

Whatever you do, you should always ask the Lord daily to bless the works of your hands and to make your employment successful. In the Lord's Prayer, Jesus said, "Give us this day our daily bread" (Matt. 6:11). The term "daily bread" refers not only to food, but to sustenance in general. You must agree with the promise that God will bless your work.

2. GOD BLESSES THOSE WHO SUPPORT THE POOR AND NEEDY

There are several significant promises of provision for a person who cares for and helps those who are truly poor and in need. I realize that in our society there are numerous people who are either lazy or willfully incompetent, and who use the system to get as much free assistance as possible. Others have addictions or other problems that hinder them from holding a job. These are not the poor and needy I am referring to.

Some people are truly poor, and these are the people who need assistance. This is especially true in third world countries where famine, drought, and poverty are the way of life for many. In some nations of the world, the people live on less than the equivalent of one dollar a day. They live in cardboard houses, have no clean water, barely survive on small amounts of food, and have no access to health care. Every American is wealthy by comparison.

Numerous Scriptures reveal how blessings are released for those who care for the poor.

> *"He who has pity on the poor lends to the LORD,*
> *And He will pay back what he has given."*
>
> – Prov. 19:17 (NKJV)

> *"He who gives to the poor will not lack,*
> *But he who hides his eyes will have many curses."*
>
> – Prov. 28:27 (NKJV)

"He has dispersed abroad,
He has given to the poor;
His righteousness endures forever;
His horn will be exalted with honor."

– PSALM 112:9 (NKJV)

To personally illustrate how the Lord will pay back what you give to the poor, years ago, our ministry needed over one million dollars for new television equipment. As I was reading Proverbs 19:17, I was suddenly aware that God's favor would be released upon the ministry if we would assist the poor. I was inspired to begin a special fund called the Samaritan Fund, which is the tithe (ten percent) from all non-designated donations, and use it to support legitimate ministries we know that are feeding the poor and helping those in need. (We must know those who are laboring among us so that our money is not wasted.) I knew from Scripture that the Lord would repay us for sowing into the lives of the poor.

After I made out the first checks to assist several ministries, a Christian brother came on the scene, and he was able to make contacts for our necessary television equipment. He saved us over four hundred thousand dollars on the equipment. I related this savings to the favor of God for assisting the poor.

Many times when we are in financial need in the ministry, I will tell our book keeper to get more seed in the ground of those groups we personally know that are helping the needy. It is not just about releasing a seed to receive a harvest. There are ministries that depend upon our monthly support, and some have said they would need to shut their doors without those offerings.

When Christ told the rich young ruler to sell what he had and give the money to the poor and follow Him, the young businessman went away sad because he had great wealth (Matt. 19:16-22). Christ told him that he would have treasure in heaven (v-21). This young man said he had followed the law and commandments of God, but Christ said that to be perfect, he should give his wealth away (v-21). It appears this young man was trusting in his riches (1 Tim. 6:17). If he understood the Scriptures, he would have known that God would provide for him if he supported the poor, as he would be "lending unto the Lord" (Prov. 19:17).

In my town is an elderly Christian man who is quite wealthy. As a young teenager he did not have much, but he sold newspapers and gave the money for world missions and support of those in need. He continued to be a giver to the poor and to world evangelism. He eventually went into business, and it became one of the most successful businesses in our city. It seemed that he had great favor with everyone he met, and people liked his moral and business integrity. Today he is worth millions of dollars. The seed he planted for the poor when he was younger became his harvest when he was older. One of the ways God can impart unexpected blessings is when you release a portion of what you have to bless those who have nothing.

3. GOD PROVIDES THROUGH YOUR GIFTS AND INVENTIONS

Here is an interesting verse from the 1611 King James Bible:

> *"I wisdom dwell with prudence, and find out knowledge of witty inventions."*
>
> – PROV. 8:12

Since my teenage years, technology has moved from home landline telephones to cordless phones to cell phones, from mainframe computers that took up all the space in a large room to desktop computers, then to laptop computers, and then to iPads and smartphones. I remember phonograph records, Beta and VHS tapes, and cassettes. Today we have direct downloads, CDs, DVDs and Blu- Ray. Next year at this time, there will be even more new technology as the things we are using now become outdated.

Somebody invented the technology for these systems. Just the Internet alone has turned certain entrepreneurs into millionaires or billionaires in a short time. Consider eBay, Facebook and Google to name just a few.

One way God creates provision for you is by using the untapped gifts that reside in your mind or in your hands. Let us consider a few gifts that have brought additional income to the person possessing these abilities. People who love to cook might run catering businesses on the side. Individuals gifted in hospitality and travel services are paid a commission for their services. Others have dynamic personalities and are experts in setting up meetings and connecting people. Individuals work on the side and make income from graphic and computer technology, programming, writing for ministries and businesses, and so on.

Previously I mentioned that I began writing songs years ago. Through my contacts I have been blessed to have over forty songs recorded and have received royalty checks for them. Then, after many years of writing books, I was approached to write under a contract for a major publisher, which enabled me to have extra income through the advance for writing the book.

Pam and I have a friend who worked for the ministry years ago, booking meetings, arranging the details, and helping set the budget. On two occasions, we were either overcharged or experienced a situation where we had to pay for things that were already included in the contract price. This young woman had such a dynamic personality in dealing with people that, in both situations, she came out of the meeting with thousands of dollars in savings for the ministry.

We teased her that she was like Esther in the Bible when she stood before the king and had favor. Her ability to smooth over difficult situations and obtain favor was a gift that either a person has or does not have. If you cannot deal with people, or if you are brash, short tempered, and stink the atmosphere when you depart, then you are void of the gift of hospitality and should find a job where you are more gifted.

By discovering your God-given gifts, you can use them as a means of providing additional income—and in some cases, primary income—for you and your family.

4. GOD BLESSES BY UNTAPPED DISCOVERIES

The fourth and rather unusual manner in which God gives provision is through untapped discoveries. One example comes from a kibbutz in Israel.

On the western shore of the Sea of Galilee is the Ginosar Kibbutz. In 1986 a drought struck Israel, causing the Sea of Galilee waters to recede. Beams of wood were seen protruding from the waters, which were discovered to be the remains of a two-thousand-year old boat! A double rainbow appeared on the day it was found and a moonbow appeared during the rescue. Inside the old remains were oil lamps, coins, pots and potsherds. The question was, what can we do with the remains of this old boat?

As news reports spread around the world, interest in seeing the boat spread among tourists visiting Israel. The kibbutz made a decision to restore the boat and open a business where viewers could see the boat, hear the story, eat and shop. Today, practically every tour bus that comes to Israel has the Jesus Boat—also called the Galilee Boat—on the itinerary! Who could imagine that tapping into an untapped discovery would bring millions of tourists, along with their money, to a farming community and a region where Christ once ministered!

I have traveled to Israel since 1985. Each year our groups tour the remains of Capernaum, where Christ often ministered in the Galilee. Our tour guide would always point to a pile of dirt and show us where Magdela, the home town of Mary Magdalene once stood. A few years ago, after settling a land dispute, archeologists began excavating. Today this is where one of the finest archeological sites in Israel is being developed. The plans are to build a hotel, gift shops, and a restaurant. The actual synagogue from Christ's time has been discovered, along with the remains of the entire city. This site will become a favorite destination and eventually bring in millions of tourists dollars. The money for their future was buried in the dirt of centuries, and by tapping into a hidden discovery, income is provided.

The same was true when, in 1947, a young Arab shepherd boy discovered jars in a cave that held the famous Dead Sea Scrolls. At the time of their discovery the entire area was barren, desolate and rocky. There was no reason to travel there except to see the Dead Sea. Today there is a major tourist attraction called the Qumran Village with a restaurant and shops, and the area is prosperous. What was in the *ash* brought in the *cash*!

One of the most astonishing stories involves one of my friends in Israel. They are Christian Arabs and have been living in the Holy Land for many years. In their earlier days, the family sold water, soda, candy and postcards to tourists. One day the head of the family began asking the Lord to help and bless them as they were living in the land of the Bible and in a city that is special to Christ. The family was growing, and they decided to expand their home. He felt impressed to draw a line on the ground and dig the footers.

As they dug deep, they found a wooden box filled with Turkish gold coins! The coins were valued at over five million dollars. This find enabled them to build an olive wood factory and several shops in the area, which support both their family as well as many Christian Arabs in the area.

5. GOD BLESSES BY UNEXPECTED BLESSINGS

Some time back I was reading the narrative in Acts 3 of Peter and John entering the Temple and being stopped by a lame man who asked for money. Peter instructed the man to "look on us," and the fellow looked up, perhaps expecting to receive money. Instead, he received healing for his body. I have often said the man was "begging for alms and got a new set of legs instead!"

I was struck by the word "expecting," and realized that expectancy is the key to receiving an unexpected blessing—unexpected referring to a source that you are not looking to for assistance. I sensed a stirring in my spirit and the Holy Spirit began to speak to me and say, "Many of the Lord's children go to His house to worship and go through the routine week after week and never expect a spiritual blessing or breakthrough. They attend by habit without ever expecting a visitation from heaven. They have maintained a routine of giving, but have lost the faith to believe that the Lord will bless them, and often from an unexpected source.

In North America particularly, believers become so accustomed to a routine that we lose the childlike expectancy and excitement we once had. We attend church, go through the routine of worship, drop the tithe or offering into the bucket, and hope the minister stops preaching by noon to ensure we get to the local restaurant before the crowd. Thus, we experience the routine without expecting a different outcome.

When the Holy Spirit revealed this simple truth to me, I had a strong inspiration (or impression) that I should begin to share this with people in our conferences. So I started telling people that when they give, they should expect unexpected blessings from unexpected sources. The Holy Spirit led me to announce that the entire month of March would be a season connected to the coming feasts of Israel and a time to give a ministry offering with *expectation*. During my entire ministry, neither I nor my staff has ever witnessed such unusual and sudden breakthroughs for the people who responded to the word.

One minister gave fifty dollars in the offering and three days later was handed a check for five thousand dollars from a businessman who was not a member of his church, but felt impressed to write a check. Others received unexpected pay raises, insurance checks, sales of homes and property in a stagnant market, and countless other unexpected blessings from unexpected sources. One young man needed money to pay his apartment rent and was down to his last quarter. He *volunteered* at no charge to work a weekend at a church he had never attended, and the church gave him an unexpected check for a thousand dollars, which was enough for three payments instead of just one.

I told each congregation the Word that was in my spirit, but I reminded them that they must believe the Word and sense it deep in their spirit before acting upon it. We cannot do something simply for the sake of doing it, or try it just to see if it works, as there is no expectancy in your actions.

God's blessings come in seasons, meaning at a specific set time. These blessing are released as doors of friendship, relationships, and opportunities are opened. Heaven has its own doors that open, bringing blessings from God to earth. The Lord told Malachi that He would "open up the windows of heaven and pour you out a blessing" (Mal. 3:10). Jesus spoke to His disciples that they would see "heaven open and angels ascend and descend" upon him (John 1:51). John looked upward from his island prison on Patmos and in a vision he "saw a door in heaven open" (Rev. 4:1). Later in the vision, he viewed the future return of Christ and wrote, "I saw heaven opened..." (Rev. 19:11). We use the term that "a door was opened" to mark the special opportunities that arise in our lives.

There is a spiritual principle of the *season*. One of the Hebrew words for season is *mowed* and refers to the special seasons ordained by God, including the yearly cycle of the feasts, monthly new moons and weekly Sabbaths. For a believer, there can be seasons of spiritual temptation and testing, as indicated when Satan tempted Jesus for forty days. Then Satan departed from Jesus for a season, meaning he would return later, at a more opportune time (Luke 4:13).

Blessings are also released in seasons, as Paul revealed, "We shall reap in due season if we do not faint (Gal. 6:9). The parable of the faithful and wise servant identifies those faithful to the Lord who will be rewarded in due season. The phrase "due season" is used ten times in the Bible. To me, a "due" season is when the time for something to happen has arrived. When a bill is due, it means it is time to pay up. When your due season comes, it marks the moment that blessings are about to be released.

Abraham at age seventy-five received a promise from God that he would become a great nation and have a son. His wife Sarah was biologically unable to give birth. Twenty-four years later, when Abraham was ninety-nine (Gen 17:1) and Sarah was eighty-nine, God visited them and confirmed the promise of a son named Isaac (Gen. 18).

When Sarah laughed at the promise, the Lord reminded her, "Is anything too hard for the LORD?" Then God said, "At the appointed time I will return to you, according to the time of life, and Sarah shall have a son" (Gen 18:14). God waited until it was impossible for Sarah to give birth to demonstrate His miraculous ability to cause the barren womb to sing (Isa. 54:1). Thus, God has an appointed time, a due season, in which to manifest His promise. Abraham and Sarah were required to stand in faith without wavering to experience their due season—in due season!

Who would have expected the birth of a child at their ages? However, like Abraham learned, our God is the God of the impossible, and the initiator of the unexpected blessings.

A person can give tithes and offerings and expect God to bless them (Mal. 3:10; Luke 6:38). Yet, so many believers withhold their financial gifts for a church, ministry outreach, or evangelism in general because of the recession or fear of lack in their future. If believers really believed that God is able and willing to return their giving in even greater measure, they would never hesitate to release finances for the Kingdom.

After we received ministry offerings and asked men and women to give with expectancy and believe God for the unexpected blessing, we received hundreds of testimonies confirming that the Lord watched over His word and performed it (Jer. 1:12). In our obedience, we should follow the instructions of the Lord, just as we follow the instructions of those over us in the workplace. Just as you expect a reward for your hard work, you can expect God's attention on your behalf for your faithful obedience.

6. PROVISION FROM THE HAND OF YOUR ENEMY

God's provision is found on a road of faith that is paved with the power of prayer. Trust and confidence in the Almighty places you in the direction of provision as you understand God's amazing ability to intervene in the affairs of men, even interrupting their routine to bring unexpected resources for His covenant people.

While this is an uncommon concept to consider, it is possible that some of the provision for your vision and some of the seed to meet your need may be released from the hand of a person who is opposed to you. Provision can come from your own enemy, even without their knowledge. One example involves the weapons the children of Israel used in battle after they departed from Egypt. This often overlooked miracle is reported by the Jewish historian Josephus.

When Moses led the Hebrews from Egypt, there were six hundred thousand men on foot (Exod. 12:37) and countless women and children. The Hebrew men departed with their clothes and personal possessions, but had no weapons, as they were exiting Egypt as a unit of slaves who were previously owned by the Pharaoh of Egypt. These fathers and their sons had never fought in any battle, and Pharaoh would have never provided weapons to former slaves, especially considering that he later chased them down with six hundred chariots; and according to Josephus in Book II, chapter XV, Pharaoh acquired the strength of 50,000 horsemen and 200,000 footmen who were all armed.

Israel departed without weapons in Exodus chapter 12; but by chapter 16 these same Hebrew men were fighting in a war with a large tribe called Amalek. The question becomes, where did Israel obtain weapons for their battle?

When reading this narrative I was aware of the Hebrews "spoiling the Egyptians," prior to their departure (Exod. 12:36), and their plunder consisted of gold and silver jewels that they took from the Egyptians (Ps. 105:37). These valuable commodities would be given for an offering to construct the tabernacle in the wilderness and provide gold for the sacred furniture (Exod. 35:5). There is no report of any Egyptian soldier giving up swords or spears to these Hebrews, and in the minds of the Hebrews, they were simply headed back to the Promised Land.

Under normal circumstances, the journey should have taken only a few weeks. God directed the Israelites through the wilderness to avoid the land of the Philistines, who were fully armed with weapons. God knew that the Hebrews would see war and desire to return to Egypt (Exod. 13:17). These were 600,000 men with a *slave* and not a *soldier* mentality, trained to make mud bricks and not fight with swords and spears.

It is the Jewish historian Josephus who gives us great insight into the question, where did the Hebrew's get their weapons after departing from Egypt? The answer is that God gave the Israelites the weapons of their enemies. Josephus stated that Pharaoh led his army of charioteers to the edge of the mighty Red Sea. As the army entered the sea, the walls of water closed over them, drowning the entire Egyptian army. In the morning the bodies of the Egyptian soldiers washed upon the shore. The Biblical account reads:

"Thus the Lord saved Israel that day out of the hand of the Egyptians and Israel saw the Egyptians dead upon the sea shore."

— EXODUS 14:30

Josephus revealed that the weapons of the Egyptians also washed upon the shore of the sea. The Hebrews stripped the dead bodies of their enemies and picked up the weapons that were lying upon the shore line. Here is the quote from Josephus:

> "On the next day Moses gathered together the weapons of the Egyptians, which were brought to the camp of the Hebrews by the current of the sea, and the force of the winds resisting it; and he conjectured that this also happened by Divine Providence, that so that they might not be destitute of weapons. So when he ordered the Hebrews to arm themselves with them, he led them to Mount Sinai in order to offer sacrifice to God, and to render oblations for the salvation of the multitude, as he was charged to do beforehand."
>
> — JOSEPHUS, ANTIQUITIES OF THE JEWS: BOOK II; CHAP. XV

Normally, iron (such as an iron weapon) would sink in the water as the ax head did when the son of a prophet was chopping down a tree in the time of Elisha (2 Kings 6:4-5); however through divine intervention the iron floated to the surface (2 Kings 6:6). The miracle at the Red Sea was that heavy weapons that would normally sink were found washed ashore and transferred from the Egyptian soldiers to the hands of former slaves now ready for battle. The weapons that were intended to kill the Hebrews became weapons for them to defeat future enemies.

In the Hebrew exodus, there was a gap of time between their *physical departure* and their actual *entrance* into the Promised Land. During this transition, there were specific needs—food, water, warmth from the cold nights, protection from serpents, and health care needs in this dry, desolate desert. It required total trust in the Almighty with the belief that supernatural provision would be provided from the beginning to the end of the journey.

The Body of Christ (and the world) has entered a time identified prophetically as the time of the end (Dan. 8:17; 12:4, 9), the last days

(2 Tim. 3:1; 2 Pet. 3:3), and the latter times (1 Tim. 4:1). These terms identify the seasons prior to the initiation of the Great Tribulation (Matt. 24:21) and the return of the Messiah to rule and reign on earth for a thousand years (Rev. 20:4). During the days prior to the great departure of the overcoming saints (Revelation chapters 2-3) to heaven, there will be times of spiritual, social, moral and economic upheavals. During these difficult times, believers must understand the promises of God and how God can and will use whatever means necessary to provide for the needs of His covenant people.

As we saw in the case of the ancient Hebrew nation, God provided from a very unusual source. He provided the weapons of the very enemies who intended to slay the Israelites at the Red Sea!

THE ATHEIST AND THE GROCERIES

Long before the days of air conditioning, people kept the windows of their homes opened in the summer. One day a precious elderly Christian woman was praying very loud, petitioning God for food, as she had no money for groceries and her kitchen cupboards were bare. Near her home lived an atheist who overheard her bold conversation with God. The man plotted a strategy. He would purchase groceries and give them to the woman to demonstrate that he—not God—provided for her.

Not long after the woman prayed, she heard a knock on her door. There stood the atheist with bags of groceries. The elderly woman raised her hands and began to shout, "Thank you Lord! Thank you Jesus! Oh, praise God!"

The atheist replied, "God had nothing to do with this. I am the one who bought the groceries and not God, because there is no God! I heard you praying and wanted to prove to you that man and not God does these things."

The woman stopped, thought for a moment and began rejoicing again, shouting, "God did provide, and He made the devil pay for it!"

Atheists are the adversaries of Biblical truth; yet no unbelief can prevent God from fulfilling His promises for those who will believe.

When we are in covenant with God, then His adversaries become our enemies and our adversaries become His enemies. God's enemies are not *people*, just as our spiritual warfare is not against flesh and blood, but against demonic and satanic spirits (Eph 6:12). Often we believe that if a person is resisting our words, working against us, or clashing with our personality, they are an adversary and God dislikes them because we dislike them. Yet God loves the person (John 3:16), but despises the evil spirit that is working within those persons.

Jesus rebuked evil spirits and evil intent, but always ministered to those in need (Acts 10:38). God's enemies include sin, transgression, iniquity, sickness, disease, death, and the works of the flesh (Gal. 5:19-21). These too should be our enemies. Our enemies are the principalities, powers, rulers of the darkness of this world, and wicked spirits in heavenly places.

THE SWORD OF GOLIATH

When David, a teenage champion of Israel, decked Goliath by slinging a smooth stone from his slingshot, many scholars note that the rock stunned or knocked out the giant. Reading 1 Samuel 17:50, we know that David had no sword in his hand. The only weapon available to complete the assignment and slay this adversary was the giant's own sword. Please note that the very weapon intended to cut David to pieces and feed him to the birds (1 Sam. 17:44) was the same weapon David seized and used to behead Israel's enemy! This is an example of God taking something from the hand of the enemy—something meant for evil—and giving it to you to use against your adversary, thereby turning something meant for evil into something good.

7. GOD CHANGES YOUR ECONOMIC STATUS

Your greatest enemy to conquer is that of practicing a lifestyle of sin. The Gospel not only impacts your spiritual life and destiny, but it also impacts your economic status. Let me explain by using an example.

When my dear friend Floyd Lawhon was an international evangelist, he would preach each year at an inner city church called Chicago Tabernacle, pastored by Jim Steele. While ministering there in 1970, an old man slipped into the back pew during the service. His clothing was ragged and worn. His long beard and hair were matted, and his body odor was so repulsive that those near him, many whom were former street people, were becoming nauseated.

The pastor of the church had a custom. When any person came to the altar to repent, he would meet them, hug them and tell them he loved them. Often this expression of love was the first time these street people had been shown affection in many years. As this man walked toward the altar, the pastor stood to meet him. The odor was so bad that the pastor remained on the stage. As the man stood alone, the pastor suddenly surged toward him and hugged him.

Lawhon later asked the pastor, "How were you able to do that?" The pastor replied, "I couldn't do it in myself. I did it for Jesus." That night, the old man repented of his sins and asked Christ to change his life.

The following night, at the conclusion of the service, a man came forward to greet Lawhon and the pastor. He was thanking them for what God was doing. He was dressed in a suit, clean shaven, and seemed very intelligent. They didn't recognize the fellow, but to their astonishment, it was the man who had been converted the night before! He was not an old man after all, but a middle aged man who had been living on the streets. That one service radically changed his life, and he became one of the faithful members of that church.

Each year, Lawhon returned to preach an annual revival. He would notice that certain people were no longer attending the church. When he asked about them the pastor would say, "Oh, they got a good job and have moved out of the inner city into the suburbs," or, "God began to bless them and they were married and are prospering at a new job." It was clear to Lawhon that the power of the Gospel not only impacted the spiritual condition of the people, but as they grew in faith and began walking in a covenant relationship with God, their very social and economic status began to change.

HABITS COST A LOT OF MONEY

When a person receives Christ and beings to walk in the New Covenant, their entire life, including their economic status begins to change. Part of this change results in a powerful transformation of the human spirit. The power of God liberates the soul and spirit, which will eventually bring deliverance from habits of the flesh that once cost a lot of money.

Let's assume that a carton of cigarettes costs about fifty dollars, and a six-pack of beer costs about six dollars. If a man went to a club every weekend, he could waste fifty dollars or more. A drug addict might spend a hundred dollars a week and more on their addiction. If you smoke a carton of cigarettes a week and drink two six-packs of beer, that is nearly $250 a month that you spend on those two habits. This cost could double or triple in other parts of the country with higher cigarette taxes. Think how much money a person could save each week by giving up these two habits.

Occasionally in a service, I ask people how much they used to spend each weekend to have what they considered a "good time" sinning. The average amount seemed to be about $250 a weekend. This means that the average person could spend as much as a thousand dollars a month on sin, habits or addictions. What could the average person do with an additional thousand dollars a month? One man, a former drug addict, told me that he spent thousands of dollars *every week* when he was an addict!

The various forms of bondages and sins that lock you into a spiritual prison are actually the enemies of God. Through His powerful redemptive covenant, He can release you from those chains of captivity and free you. The weapons that were defeating you are now themselves defeated, and you can enter the future armed with knowledge, wisdom and redemption.

8. GOD CAN TRANSFER THE WEALTH OF THE SINNER

One of the most unusual stories that received national exposure and much controversy years ago was when a noted minister was attempting to raise a significant amount of money for a specific project. He was short of funds before the deadline, and an elderly man who owned a dog race track saw him on television and sent a $1.3 million donation so that he would stop asking for money. This check was large enough to provide all the funds the ministry needed.

This money came from an unusual source. The donation caused a controversy among some Christians who could not believe that a minister would take gambling money from a dog track owner. Others just smiled and said, "Well, the Bible says that the wealth of the sinner is laid up for the just" (Prov. 13:22).

I have pondered this incident and have a few comments to make concerning money in general. Money is amoral, meaning that it is neither good nor bad. We all know that money is necessary to pay for housing, transportation, food, utilities, medical expenses, education and so on. It is also a fact that some of the older hundred dollar bills have traces of cocaine on them. However, are you going to throw away your Benjamin Franklins because of that?

The Bible says that the *love of money* is the root of all evil (1 Tim. 6:10); but it is the *need or desire* for money that motivates some criminals to steal from others.

Money in the hands of a wicked person will enable them to do wicked things. The same amount of money in the hands of a righteous person becomes a resource to be a blessing to their family and others. It is the same money, but used in two opposite ways. In the hands of a sinner it can become filthy lucre, which is a phrase found in four passages of Scripture that alludes to getting money in a sordid, illegal or immoral manner (1 Tim. 3:3, 8; Titus 1:7; 1 Pet. 5:2). It also can refer to a person who is greedy for their own personal gain. When Simon the magician offered Peter money for the gift of the Holy Spirit, Peter reprimanded the man for the iniquity in his heart (Acts 8:18-22) and told him to repent.

When money of any kind is taken from the hands of sinners and placed in the hands of believers, that money is then sanctified by the believer. The money itself is only paper or coinage. The use of the money is the most important factor. Thus, when the minister received the large donation, the money was then used for the ministry and not for some carnal or sordid purpose. It is far better that money be in the hands of those who will use it for the Lord's purposes.

CHAPTER 8

Breaking the Fear of Financial Provision for the End Time

Two things torment people: the guilt of yesterday and the fear of tomorrow. Guilt will paralyze your *confidence* in your own prayers (1 John 3:21-23). Fear will paralyze your confidence in God's *willingness* to be your provider and answer your prayers.

There are three major fears most people will encounter during their lifetime. The ultimate fear is the fear of death. Paul spoke of "those who through fear of death were all their lifetimes subject to bondage" (Heb 2:15). The second fear is fear of a sickness that would snuff out your life prematurely. This could be why the top selling books in America are ones dealing with how to live a long and be free from disease and sickness. The third and very powerful fear is that of being unable to provide for your personal needs, including needs such as paying the mortgage and other bills, or providing for your retirement.

One of Christ's parables reveals the thinking of certain servants who were given a portion of their master's money to invest. Two of the men made wise investments and doubled the money, causing them to be called "profitable servants" (Matt. 25:20-23). The third servant was considered an unprofitable servant because of what he did with the master's money. When the master came to take account, he discovered that this servant had hidden the money in the ground. When asked why, he responded:

"So I was afraid, and I went and hid your talent in the ground. Here you have what is your own."

– Matt. 25:25 (AMP)

Fear forged a negative motivation and instead of investing the money and gaining interest, this servant's fear caused him to hide the investment money. We have all heard of older people whose families lost money during the Great Depression, who amassed wealth and hid cash in odd places out of fear of losing it. True stories have been told of people who discovered tens and hundreds of thousands of dollars hidden in the walls of someone's home after their death. Some elderly people who have large bank accounts will not spend one penny because of the fear that sometime in the future, they might need the money.

Before continuing, it must be pointed out that Christ conquered all three fears on behalf of mankind. He conquered death, He defeated and cured diseases, and He provided food when He multiplied loaves and fishes and turned water to wine at a wedding. He even provided tax money for Himself and Peter. Second Timothy 1:7 says that God has not given us a spirit of fear. This tells us that fear is a spirit, and it is not a spirit that comes from the Almighty.

THE ROOT CAUSE OF FEAR

The root cause of fear is insecurity. The need for security is a basic human instinct, and one must feel secure to have a sense of inner peace. But what if you lived your entire life in fear? Perhaps you would be unable to sleep at night for fear the house could burn down. You would never fly because the plane could crash and kill you. If you fear gaining weight, you might become bulimic or anorexic. Since it is possible that you could attend church and become offended and hurt by someone, you add church to your list of places to avoid.

Here's the big one: you never tithe or give in an offering because you fear that you might need the money later. It is fear of not having provision that restrains a person from being a generous giver to the work of the Kingdom of God. Many believers are unbelievers when it comes to *believing* that God can give back to them what they have planted into God's Kingdom in the form of financial gifts.

FINANCIAL STRUGGLES ARE NOTHING NEW

To understand how and why God provided for the material and financial needs of His covenant children in the Old Testament, we must understand the economic and cultural setting of the early times. The early nation of Israel, until the time of Christ, had at least six ways of earning income.

The Sea of Galilee was a large lake of water in the central part of northern Israel, where small cities had been established around the lake because of the fishing industry. Many of Christ's disciples were fishermen and some owned their own boats (Matt. 4:18-22). The Mediterranean Sea was a coastal area running north from Lebanon to Gaza in the south, allowing for industries such as shipping and ports that were located in places such as Joppa and Caesarea.

In central Israel were thousands of farms that provided produce that was consumed by the local population and, at times, carted to other cities or shipped by boat to surrounding, close nations.

Jerusalem and the Bethlehem area were both known as religious centers. In Jerusalem, the Temple, the priests, and the sacrifices provided much of the economic activity. A strong olive and olive oil industry was linked with Jerusalem and Bethlehem.

The area toward Hebron was known for the wine industry and grape vineyards which produced some of the most desirable grapes in that part of the world. Even the twelve spies were so impressed that they brought back clusters of grapes so large that two men had to carry them on poles (Num. 13).

Another major industry, especially in the time of the Temple and the building programs of Herod the Great, were stone masonry and carpentry. Joseph was a carpenter according to Mark 6:3.

Thus, Israel's economic base was fishing, farming, oil, wine, grains, stone masons and builders. We can also add net makers, pottery makers, salt miners and other jobs that were important but received less recording in the Scriptures.

Had you been living in ancient Israel during both the Old Testament and the Roman period (Christ's time), you would have dealt with several things which, individually or collectively, could have destroyed the economic base for a family, business or entire nation.

There are records of no rain in Israel for forty-two months, which caused droughts and famines that were so terrible, people were eating dove's dung and donkey's heads to survive (2 Kings 6:25).

Wars and civil uprisings caused raiders to invade homes, taking valuable spoil and then burning the homes, leaving families without shelter (1 Sam. 30).

During farming season there was always a threat of locusts and pestilences that could destroy entire fields of precious crops, leaving a farmer without food or income. Each year financial pressure fell upon the breadwinner of the house as Roman taxes, temple taxes, and tolls were charged to help build roads, provide for the Roman army, and repair the Temple.

As far back as Old Testament days, people dealt with financial woes that were sometimes caused by situations over which they had little or no control. These things will happen, and many times we can do nothing to change them. This is why, if you are a believer who is in covenant with God, you must learn to depend on God to provide for you supernaturally.

SUPERNATURAL PROVISION

The word supernatural brings different images to the minds of people, and some believers hesitate to use the word, even when speaking about the power of God to intervene. Natural provision comes from the hands, work and ability of men, but supernatural provision comes when God works in an unusual and unexplainable manner to create something we do not have in order to bring forth something we need.

In the Old Testament, a widow woman and her son were dying and the prophet requested that she prepare him the last cake of meal she had. She obeyed and the supernatural result was that her meal barrel never ran dry throughout the entire famine. We read:

> "...She and her household ate for many days. The bin of flour was not used up nor did the jar of oil run dry, according to the word of the Lord which he spoke by Elijah."
>
> – 1 KINGS 17:15-16 (NKJV)

On another occasion a widow woman owed her mortgage and could not pay. The creditors sent a final notice and informed her that her two sons would be sold as slaves to provide the payment for the home. The woman knew the prophet Elisha, and sought him for divine assistance. The prophet instructed her to take the oil remaining in her house, borrow vessels, and shut the door. After prayer the vessels were filled and the women sold the oil, made her house payment, and lived off the rest of the income.

Josephus makes an interesting observation about the husband of this woman. He was Obediah, the former governor of Ahab's house, who feared God and had hidden one hundred prophets in two caves, feeding them bread and protecting them from Jezebel's assassination attempt. The historian writes that, in order to feed the prophets, Obediah took out a loan against his house to purchase bread and feed these men of God who were in hiding (1 Kings 18:4).

Years passed. As the government financial records in Samaria were being checked, they noticed the loan had never been paid back, as Obediah had died before repaying it. Creditors came to collect and the widow of Obediah cried out for supernatural intervention (2 Kings 4:1). Josephus wrote:

> "For they say that the widow of Obediah, Ahab's steward, came to him and said he was not ignorant how her husband had preserved the prophets that were to be slain by Jezebel...he borrowed money for their maintenance and after her husband's death she and her children were carried away to be made slaves by creditors..."
>
> – JOSEPHUS BOOK IX, CHAPTER IV

Elisha, being a servant of Elijah, knew how Obediah had fed the prophets, so he now sought God on behalf of his widow. Obediah's obedience did more than spare the prophets in times of famine; he also built a spiritual memorial in heaven (Acts 10:1-4), enabling his wife to tap into a special favor and blessing, even when the man had passed away. God remembered her for her husband's faithfulness.

PRACTICAL AND BIBLICALLY-BASED INSTRUCTION

In this section are several practical and Biblically-based methods to assist you in making right decisions regarding your debt and finances.

1. WHAT IS IN YOUR HOUSE?

The Lord asked Moses what was in his hand and Elisha asked the widow woman what was in her house. When the Lord marks you for supernatural provision, he will often use something that you have to create something you need.

When I felt the call into the ministry as a sixteen year old minister's son, I was good friends with an older minister who was also a writer and a book printer. At age eighteen my personal desire was to write a small 32-page book, but what subject can an eighteen-year-old write about? I had few life experiences and limited Biblical knowledge. However, I did understand and believe in the Biblical promises of God for believers. By faith I wrote a manuscript called "Precious Promises for Believers." The next challenge was to find the money to print five hundred books.

I had something in my house that the printer was interested in buying for his son. From age eleven to eighteen, I played the drums. Now that I was traveling I would no longer need a drum set. The printer and I agreed that if I would give him my drum set, he would lay out and print five hundred copies of the book.

Although I was by no means the next C. S. Lewis, within thirty days I had in hand my first booklet to sell. This one act initiated that which would, years later, become the Voice of Evangelism Outreach—a worldwide ministry that touches 180 nations of the world.

Consider what you might have in your possession that can be used to provide provision through sale or trade.

2. LEARN TO SAVE MONEY

Americans are spenders and not savers, but we need to discipline ourselves and learn to save money. One way to save is to ask yourself if your purchase is a want or a need. Americans buy too much on credit, and anything bought on credit has a due date. If the bill isn't paid in full by the due date, interest charges can easily build up to the point that half your monthly payment is going toward interest charges. The borrower can easily become shackled to the lender; and as the bills pile up, so does the stress.

It is always wise to train yourself to pay as you go as much as possible, and this requires discipline—both in making purchases and in putting aside money for the future.

I have discovered that the more cash you have in your pocket, the more tempted you will be to spend it for things you might not need. Whether eating in a restaurant, shopping or going on vacation, make a budget. Write a list of items you need, figure out how much you can spend, and stay within that budgeted amount.

3. SELL, DON'T HOARD

Do not hoard your belongings when you can sell some of them to assist your family with additional income. Today there are numerous ways to sell items that years ago did not exist. Many people simply throw something in a garage sale. But people who purchase in this manner expect the seller to practically give away their items. If you have a nice and rather costly object, you will lose money selling it in a garage or yard sell.

Today many sales are transacted through Internet sites such as eBay, or for high quality art, antiques and rare collectibles, sites such as WorthPoint. Sometimes listing items in the city newspaper or a local trade paper will net you a good price. Local auctions are another option. With an auction, at times you might bring in less than you expect, while other times you will receive more than you expect.

Years ago I purchased about eighty silver spoons for seventy dollars. Just one of those spoons was sold on eBay for seven hundred dollars. I had no idea when I purchased it that it was a rare spoon from the 1800s. Another time I spent about ten dollars purchasing a few nice old pictures at a yard sale, and later I sold them at an auction and received about fifty dollars. At auctions, small items are sold last and often in bulk if there are many similar items. Very little profit is made in these bulk sales. Auctions produce better income for items such as antiques, furniture, collectibles, and miscellaneous items that have value. Other methods are better for selling small items.

May I also suggest that you not sell something that could be valuable if you are uncertain of its worth. Occasionally someone will place a family heirloom in an auction and discover that something they sold for five dollars was actually worth five hundred dollars. Do your research, either through books or online, to determine a fair value for your item before you sell it.

When you are selling expensive merchandise, especially electronics or nice jewelry, be careful when shipping overseas. Scams that originate in certain countries—particularly Nigeria—have caused people to lose both their item and their money. Here is how they generally work. You will receive an email notification from PayPal telling you that the item has sold, and oftentimes the seller is paying extra for express shipping. The problem is this: the PayPal notification is fraudulently created to make it appear that it came from PayPal when it did not. People ship the item, and by the time they discover the fraud, the item is in the hands of the scam artist.

Anytime you are shipping an expensive item or an overseas order to someone you do not know (particularly in Nigeria), always check the sale through your PayPal account to make certain the item was indeed sold and the payment processed. Do not depend on the email as verification. Use caution if you accept credit cards, too, as much fraudulent activity involves stolen credit card information.

I am not implying that you will get rich by selling things second-hand, but this is a great way to help you earn extra income. While some things simply do not sell well in a downturned economy because people are more cautious about how they spend their money, today we are blessed to have a variety of avenues for selling merchandise. Gain some knowledge and do your research in advance so you will know what is selling, what to buy for resale, and the value of the items you are selling. Even this requires wisdom if you hope to make money.

4. SELLING GOLD JEWELRY

With the price of gold today, it is wise to consider the value of any gold jewelry you might no longer be using, and how it could be sold for extra income.

Here is a word of caution. You will see countless television commercials from companies suggesting that you send them your unwanted gold jewelry for instant cash. These companies instruct you to fill out a form, mail your jewelry in a secure package, and expect a check in a few days or weeks. In my opinion, this is an unwise way of selling your jewelry because you do not know the people with whom you are dealing. If you are sending jewelry that contains diamonds or other gemstones, you might not get them back when you send in your gold jewelry for cash. The company will then have your gold, as well as your diamonds and gemstones that can be sold to an outside source.

In my opinion and that of others, a person should never mail valuables to an unknown company in this manner, as most companies never tell you how they are evaluating the cost of your gold. There is 10, 14, 18 and 24 karat gold jewelry; the higher the karat, the purer and more valuable the gold. A company can tell you that your shipment was worth only a certain amount, and if you did not know how to weigh the jewelry on a jewelers scale and understand its quality, you could get twenty-five to seventy percent less than you should be receiving.

Here are two examples I know of from sources in my home town. A group of men came to a hotel in our community and advertised that they would give the highest price possible for scrap gold. A widow woman brought her husband's gold Rolex watch. The "gold expert" told her that he could give her only $350. She was happy to receive that amount. However, she later learned from an honest person in the community that the watch was worth about $4,000!

Another young woman took a few rings into a shop that purchased gold and was told the rings were worth seventy dollars. They also told her this included her diamonds in the ring. She then took it to a Christian friend of mine who weighed the ring, gave her double for the gold, and told her to sell the diamonds separately for about $600. I call some of these dealers the "scrap jewelry con men."

A person who plans to sell their jewelry should research the important information in advance and receive several estimates. If possible, do business face to face. Ask a knowledgeable friend to accompany you, especially if you might be perceived as an easy target. Also be aware that you will never receive the price that you originally paid for your jewelry when you sell it in this manner. You might receive one fourth of the original price when selling to someone who plans to resell it. Selling to another individual without a middle man could bring you a better price.

5. SPEND WISELY

Another important principle is to learn to spend wisely. It is important in business, ministry and personal life to find as many ways as possible to save money and thereby protect your income.

In our ministry, we have a weekly telecast that costs $4.4 million dollars a year for air time on over seventy stations and networks. This is about $370,000 a month or $85,000 a week. When we began to negotiate contracts in the late 1990s, we learned several important things. First, many networks pay a certain percentage to agents that are hired to purchase air time for a client. This percentage is automatically in the rate quoted by the station. Second, many stations are concerned about a client paying their bills on time, and if a client will pay in advance, a discount is often given.

Since my office manager and I were personally involved in purchasing the air time with no agent involved, I asked the stations to deduct the percentage in the price quoted that would be given to an agent. We then told each station that we would pay one year in advance on the condition of an additional discount. We also requested special pricing if we were on all of the network's stations, and not just the larger ones in the cities. Through this, we were able to save the ministry hundreds of thousands of dollars. Also, by paying a year in advance, we keep ourselves from receiving and paying dozens of different bills every month. This also opens the door to other networks, as we are not a risk to carry.

Another problem that happens occasionally is that, when a person gets in hand a large sum of money—perhaps through a business deal, an inheritance, a large bonus and so on, the person unwisely goes on a spending spree. They might buy new clothes, a new car, new furniture, a larger home and so on. Then later they wish they had kept the money because when they need it, they don't have it. Perhaps they experience a job layoff or some other emergency that they were unprepared for.

Spending wisely includes shopping for a good deal on personal and household goods. My wife and I were going on vacation and I needed a few items of clothing. We went to a well-known store and the items were double the price I wanted to pay. We walked down the street to a store that was having a sale, and we saved between fifty and seventy-five percent on everything.

Another way that some people save money is by using coupons. Local newspapers, especially on Sunday, offer a variety of coupons from stores and restaurants around town. Some grocery stores designate one day a week as double coupon day, and others designate a senior's discount day.

Here again is another word of caution: do not buy something just because it is on sale. Buy only what you need. Compulsive shoppers will buy something that they never use, and years later, donate it to a charity. While this is good for the charity, it is not good for your wallet.

Even grocery story couponing can get out of hand when you purchase things that you will never use. There are people who spend hours every week searching for coupons and bargains, and they might buy thirty bottles of barbeque sauce because they can purchase them for twenty cents a bottle. Again, even though it might be a bargain, why spend money on something you will never use before the expiration date? The same holds true when you find a deal that is across town. It is not wise to waste the gas to drive twenty miles just so you can save fifty cents on an item, because you spend more on gas to drive there than you save on the item.

Some of these suggestions sound like common sense that all should have, but occasionally people get their eyes set on the bargain without considering the wisdom of the purchase. Even cautious spending requires wisdom. When done properly, this principle of looking for bargains helps you save money by controlling spending. A dollar saved or a dollar not wasted is a dollar earned, because any money that you save is money that remains in your pocket. Just as your tithe is for God's storehouse (Mal. 3:10), your personal savings is for your own personal storehouse.

6. USE CAUTION WHEN LOANING MONEY

Most of us want to help friends and family as much as we possibly can, but many people have gotten themselves in a financial bind when they tried to help family members by loaning them money. Parents have lost retirement money when they loaned it to a child who never paid it back.

Proverbs 22:26-27 tells us not to enter into an agreement with somebody where we are required to put up security or collateral for a loan, because if you cannot pay it back, the lender will take your property in exchange. Proverbs 17:18 even tells us that if we put up security or collateral for a friend, we are devoid of understanding and sense. This is mentioned yet again at the beginning of Proverbs chapter 6, where the writer says that pledging to guarantee another person's debts is a snare that makes your own security subject to seizure.

If you have a friend or family member who is irresponsible and cannot handle finances, it is wise to help them work out a plan to get out of debt and learn to handle money wisely. But it is unwise to use your own money or collateral to pay the debt for them.

SEVEN THINGS THAT WILL HALT YOUR PROGRESS

The promises of provision in Scripture, as well as all New Covenant promises, manifest in the life of a believer through their individual faith and obedience. But there is a misconception that, if a person reads Scripture and believes it, the promises will automatically work—with or without any action or obedience on their part. That is not the case. I have discovered that, at times, it is our own actions that cause roadblocks to blessings. Sometimes we are our own worst enemy when it comes to succeeding at our endeavors.

Here are seven problems that will stop your progress, hinder your success, and block your financial freedom.

1. MEDIA, GAMES, AND INTERNET ADDICTION

Growing up, our entertainment was playing in the yard until dark and watching cartoons on Saturday mornings. Today, with home computers, enormous flat screen televisions, iPads that you can easily carry wherever you go, iPods, smartphones, Facebook, downloads, Internet that allows access to unlimited information and so on, it is possible to waste hours every day. People spend hours on social networking alone. They post comments and tweet to their followers if they so much as go to the mall or drink a cup of coffee. It is possible to look all around you during a church service and see people replying to texts on their phones. Texting is such an addiction that some people send a thousand texts a month. People have been killed, or been responsible for the deaths of others, all because they could not stop texting on a phone long enough to pay attention while they drive.

Young people spend entire afternoons and much of the night playing online computer games of chance, war and sports. Their day is built around the hours they can spend sitting in a chair, ignoring reality, and entering a fantasy world where they rule in a world with no rules. The fact is that these people are addicted to technology and social networking. Just as a heroin addict is constantly looking for the next fix, a media junkie cannot make it through the day without their technology.

Occasional recreational activities, games and other activities that you enjoy are necessary. But beware of time consuming addictions that pull you away from people or resources that can benefit your growth in life—including spiritual growth. Time cannot be recovered once it is gone, so do not waste it doing frivolous things. Look at your day and consider how much time you spend on computer games, television, Internet, social networking, texting and so on. Don't allow this to become an addiction. Unless your job involves the Internet or some other form of media, limit your time on these and use it toward something productive.

Spend time reading, speaking with knowledgeable people, and learning skills that you can apply toward success. If you waste your time on these addictions, you will become a sluggard who will come to poverty according to Proverbs 6:9-11.

2. PROCRASTINATION

A procrastinator puts off for another day something that needs to be done now. They are talkers but not doers. Things they should be doing lose out to things that are unimportant or even unnecessary. People who procrastinate appear lazy, and anybody who appears to be lazy will have fewer opportunities for work and advancement. I have seen people procrastinate until the last minute, and then ask for prayer that they will complete the project on time.

Some people deal with procrastination by forcing themselves to work on the most difficult task first and save the easy things for last. This is easier when you break the project into small tasks and complete it one piece at a time. Procrastination is overcome by determination, and by forcing yourself to do whatever it is that you keep putting off. Keep track of things that need to be done, and finish them in order of importance.

The person who can complete projects before the deadline will have less stress in life and be appreciated by others and noticed for promotions. Personal patterns that you establish in life will impact your work ethic. Don't put off until tomorrow what needs to be done today. Completing an assignment gives a sense of relief when it is accomplished. Make each day count and understand that you will not rise to higher levels of leadership if you are a procrastinator.

3. FINANCIAL IRRESPONSIBILITY

We have all observed different television ministers suggest that, if you will plant a certain amount of money into the ministry, you will become debt free. The fact is, even if a person were to become supernaturally debt free without learning to control their spending, they would end up in debt again. I have known people who were addicted to shopping. They purchased clothing they never wore or gadgets they never used, whether they needed these things or not. They bought anything they wanted, even if they had to charge it.

Some people are irresponsible with money and credit, but learning to be responsible with debt and finances is part of personal responsibility. Learn to live on a budget. Pay off debts and strive to live debt free. Save money by looking for bargains and foregoing the purchase of things you do not need. Do not live above your means and use a false benchmark in order to project an image and level of success you cannot afford. Those who carelessly spend and build credit will come under financial burden.

4. LACK OF DISCIPLINE IN YOUR CONVERSATION

More people have entered a fire they could not quench by opening their mouth and shooting flames toward others with words that strike the heart as burning arrows (James 3:5-6).

We have all known intelligent and well-educated people who have a hard time getting or keeping a job because of their temper, smart aleck attitude, negativity, or tendency to gossip, slander others, or give everybody a piece of their mind. Nobody wants to be around such people, unless they have the same traits and choose like-minded friends so they can commiserate with each other. If you engage in these behaviors, you will acquire a reputation that will destroy your success in life. Not only will people not want to be around you, they will go to great lengths to avoid you.

One reason successful people are successful is because they obey rules and protocol for business success, and they have a professional work ethic. They can be trusted with information. There is a time to speak and a time to be silent (Eccl. 3:7) and sometimes it is best to be silent.

A harsh word will stir up anger and the mouth of fools pours forth foolishness (Proverbs 15:1 and 2). You will never need to apologize for terrible things you did not say. Your words can always come back to haunt you in the future, so guard your tongue. If you are a person who cannot control your words and attitude, allow the Holy Spirit and the Word of God to renew both your mind and your mouth.

5. CHRONIC COMPLAINING

You never want to ask some people how they are doing. Thirty minutes later, you will know what their doctor said, what their lawyer said, how many joint pains they have, and an updated report on their rebellious child. Some people are chronic complainers. These people tend to attract other chronic complainers, and everybody else avoids the complainer because they tire of hearing them complain constantly. Often chronic complainers have a desire for personal compassion and attention, and they use their problems to draw an emotional response from the listener.

Pay attention to yourself. How are you coming across to others? Constant complaining will destroy your chances for success in life and cause you to lose friends. Allow the Holy Spirit and the Word of God to renew your mind, as well as your mouth. Speak the positive words of Scripture and your life will change. Speak a good report.

6. SELFISH BEHAVIOR

A selfish attitude says, "What's in it for me?" A selfish person is not a giver. They hoard everything for themselves and gather goods for their own plans and purposes. If you want to have success in life, instead of always taking in, you must also pour out. To take and not release demonstrates a selfish nature in which we consider ourselves more important than others.

A selfish person will never learn the joy of giving and being a blessing to others. We are blessed to be a blessing, so learn to give. Develop an attitude of working together as a team. Unselfish people who go the extra mile for others will be noticed and eventually rewarded for their efforts.

7. DEVELOPING CLOSE FRIENDSHIPS WITH THE WRONG PEOPLE

This is a great challenge for young people. You tend to become like those with whom you associate, so choose your friends carefully. Just as leaven in bread will cause it to rise, the words and actions of others will cause their bad seed to produce weeds instead of fruit. Weeds choke the life out of anything good that might grow.

If your friends are lazy, gossipers, complainers, procrastinators, immoral and so on, there is a good chance they will influence you rather than you influence them. Those who walk with wise men will be wise, and those who are the companion of fools will be destroyed (Proverbs 13:20).

CLUES YOU NEED FOR CAREER SUCCESS

People are more successful when doing something they enjoy, simply because it never seems like work, and they tend to be very good at that which they enjoy. Everybody has at least one thing they can do that will bring them joy and success in life. Every person will be happier if they discover how to find the job that enables them to both make a living and enjoy it, instead of simply doing something they don't like, just to earn a living.

How can you determine your gift that will lead to job success? Here are some clues that will help.

CLUE #1 – WHAT IS YOUR PASSION?

The burden that you carry, the desires that you have, and the passion you have for something are keys to God's direction for your life. What do you love to do? Is there something that you daydream of doing? If you could do anything you wanted to do, what would it be?

Your answer will be a clue to the direction of God's purpose for your life. You will excel at whatever that might be.

If a high school graduate has no idea what he or she wants to do in life, it might be best not to spend tens of thousands of dollars on a college education at that time. Not all young people have decided their career path by the time they are eighteen years of age, yet they are pressured to attend college just to get some kind of degree. Then they graduate and never use their degree, or wish they had chosen another major, or find themselves stuck in a minimum wage job with enormous school loans to repay. This is a controversial subject because today young people are expected to have at least one degree. But perhaps working for a couple of years or attending a trade school is a better option for some.

CLUE #2 – WHAT ARE YOUR GIFTS AND ABILITIES?

Each person is born with a gift—something they enjoy doing that seems to come naturally for them. Some are musically gifted, some are great communicators. Some have a gift of caring for the sick, or a gift of hospitality. Many of those with an entrepreneurial gift have successfully found ways to make money since they were children, no matter what they tried. Other people are great inventors. What is your gift?

A gift needs to be properly developed, and training is needed to perfect the gift. For example, you might have a creative eye for photography, but you will still need to have access to equipment, and then study to learn how to use it. The more you practice, the more talent you will have and the more likely you are to be paid well for your work.

Then expand on your gift and talent. Using photography as an example, consider other creative ideas for your pictures. They can be turned into notecards and sold for extra income. Photoshop techniques can change ordinary pictures into something that looks like impressionist or modern artwork that can be sold for additional income. Sometimes people become successful by choosing a niche, and then learning and practicing until they become known as the expert in that area. One photographer travels the world taking pictures of landscapes, and his photographs sell for hundreds and even thousands of dollars.

Your gift will make room for you. Thankfully, in this day of increased technology and availability of knowledge, you can teach yourself nearly everything you need to know. With new technology, other avenues are open to you that were not available ten years ago.

You are never too old to learn something new. Life will get boring when you think you know it all.

CLUE #3 – WHAT IS GOD'S TIMING ON THIS ISSUE?

Whatever you decide to do, be sure to pray about it and wait on God's perfect timing. Abraham had to wait twenty-five years for Isaac, the promised heir. Joseph spent seventeen years in slavery and prison before he received his breakthrough. Moses was in the desert forty years before he received his call to deliver the people from Egyptian bondage.

The Lord showed me a daughter that we would have named Amanda, but it took twelve years for her to arrive. When the Lord gave me the name *Manna-fest*, it took twelve years to birth the ministry.

The writer of Ecclesiastes wrote about the folly of riches and how that you can take nothing with you when you die. Much of what he wrote is about the enigmas of life, and he makes it clear that life without God is meaningless. But he does tell us to enjoy our labor, rejoice in it, and even receive our reward from it, for this is the gift of God:

> *"Behold that which I have seen: it is good and comely for one to eat and to drink, and to enjoy the good of all his labour that he taketh under the sun all the days of his life, which God giveth him: for it is his portion.*
>
> *"Every man also to whom God hath given riches and wealth, and hath given him power to eat thereof, and to take his portion, and to rejoice in his labour; this is the gift of God."*
>
> – Ecclesiastes 5:18-19

Determine to find your gifting and calling, so that you will rejoice in your labor and be successful in life. As the writer said, that is one of God's gifts to you!

CHAPTER 9

Breaking the Spirit of Poverty and Lack

"You have sown much, and bring in little; you eat, but do not have enough; you drink, but you are not filled with drink; you clothe yourselves, but no one is warm; and he who earns wages, earns wages to put into a bag with holes."

- HAGGAI 1:6 (NKJV)

NEW TESTAMENT CHRISTIANS tend to spend ample time reading the wisdom writings of David and Solomon, but often ignore the prophetic truths in the twelve Biblical books of the minor prophets (minor in the sense that their books have shorter texts). One of those prophets was Haggai who wrote two chapters found in the Old Testament.

Haggai was one of several prophets who ministered after the Babylonian captivity in the days of the rebuilding of the Temple under Ezra, when Zerubbabel was governor of Judea (Ezra 2:2; 3:2; 4:2-3). The Hebrew name Haggai means "my festival," causing some to suggest he may have been born during one of Israel's major feasts. He is mentioned in Ezra 5:1 and 6:14, and he wrote when the Jews had returned from Babylon and things were in a condition of deterioration.

Imagine that you had been away from your home and property for seventy years. You departed with your family as a young child, and now you are in your eighties with children and grandchildren. As you return to Israel, you arrive at your property to a heartbreaking scene. The ceiling in your former family dwelling has fallen in, and large thorn bushes and weeds are clinging to the outside stone like glue. The withered vineyards have not been pruned, and it is now your responsibility to repair this once beautiful home for you and your descendants to enjoy. It will take much time and money that you do not have.

Such was the case when, after seventy years (Jer. 25:11), the first wave of about fifty thousand Jews arrived in Judah from Babylon. Upon arrival, many were forced to borrow money from wealthy men of Israel to purchase corn, food, cattle and other animals, and to repair the home to make it livable (see Neh. 5:1-5). Haggai prophesied at the time when the Jews were repairing their homes that had fallen into disrepair. The spiritual controversy was that, as they cared for their personal needs, the repairs for the Holy Temple in Jerusalem were being ignored, to their own peril. Haggai's message reminded the people to put God's Temple first so they would gain the favor of God.

Haggai further explained why the people were not experiencing the prosperity they expected. They were sowing seed but receiving little harvest (1:6); drinking from the vineyards but remaining thirsty (1:6), and wearing clothes that were unable to warm them (1:6). The money they earned seemed to be, as we say today, going in one pocket and out the other (1:6).

Haggai reminded his people that God alone has the power to supernaturally bless and prosper them, and that God alone controls the rain. Without the rain, nothing would be productive (1:10-11). God had called for a drought to seize the attention of the people (1:11). This is referred to in Nehemiah 5:3.

ECONOMIC PARALLELS TO TODAY

Nehemiah chapter five reveals the economic condition of the people, and it is very similar to the economic crisis facing America and parts of the world today. The people were mortgaged out, as they had loans on their homes, lands and vineyards that they could not pay back (Neh. 5:2-4). The debt was being passed on to their children, and the people knew this debt was a bondage that would bring suffering in the future (Neh. 5:5). The money was being loaned by fellow Jews to other Jews with an interest rate, which was forbidden under the Law of Moses (Neh. 5:7; Deut. 23:19-20).

In North America, people have lost their homes because of the mortgage crisis. Some have had automobiles repossessed because they were unable to make payments. Unsustainable government debt is being passed to future generations, who will bear a heavy burden of government debt. The abuse by lending institutions of charging high interest on loans and credit card debt has, at times, sent families into bankruptcy. When believers are experiencing such economic stress, often the work of God suffers as people tend to withhold their giving. This was occurring in the time of Haggai and Malachi.

The prophet Malachi, also a contemporary of Haggai's, spoke of God opening the windows of heaven and pouring out a blessing—if the people would give tithe and offerings for the Temple (Mal. 3:10-11). This literally referred to rain that would bless the land. Malachi predicted that, if the people would put God's House first, they should go to the mountains and cut wood for the Temple's reconstruction (Haggai 1:1-8).

The people obeyed the prophetic word and their spirits were stirred to proceed with the building program (Haggai 1:1,12, and 15). It would have been easy for the people to become critical and accuse Haggai or Malachi of using their prophetic gift to manipulate the people. Some could have said, "He's just after our money and our time. We have our own work to do!" However, the former captives had no doubt recalled how that Nebuchadnezzar had destroyed Jerusalem, which had caused them seventy years of sorrow. They also knew that without the Creator's blessings, the heavens would be brass (Haggai 1:10) and the land, plants, trees, and even animals would wither and eventually die. If they chose to put God's house first, God promised, *"I will rebuke the devourer for your sakes, so that he will not destroy the fruit of your ground, nor shall the vine fail to bear fruit for you in the field."*

Believers who are in covenant with Christ and attend a local church must understand the spiritual principle of putting the needs of God above our own personal needs. While God Himself has no needs, the children in His Kingdom on earth experience numerous needs. There are the needs of the widows, the orphans and the fatherless; the need to feed and clothe the poor; and the need to send forth ministers to preach the Gospel to all nations. There is the need for teachers, Bibles, printed literature, prayer warriors and givers to support the ministry to reach people locally and spread the gospel globally.

All aspects of the ministry require both *laborers* and *financial givers* to support the efforts. We are told that if we seek first the kingdom of God and His righteousness that all of these things (that we need) shall be added unto us (Matt. 6:33).

When Paul was receiving special offerings for his missionary work, the church at Philippi stood with the apostle with their offerings of support. Paul thanked them and then wrote, "But my God shall supply all your need according to His riches in glory by Christ Jesus" (Phil 4:19). The prophet Haggai understood the spiritual principle of putting the House of God first, and as New Covenant believers we must also acknowledge the spiritual law of God's blessing being released when we seek first His kingdom and His righteousness!

Haggai's words were to prophesy the importance of rebuilding and repairing God's Temple in Jerusalem. Haggai, in the second chapter, reveals the difficulties the people experienced for not obeying the Lord, by showing that their harvest was cut in half and the grape vineyards were reduced from a normal fifty vessels to twenty. Mildew and hail destroyed crops. This was the warning given in the law if Israel ceased to follow God's commandments (Duet. 28:22). As they laid the foundation of the Temple, that very day, God promised that He would now bless them (Haggai 2:19) and reverse the curse!

Speaking of a curse, Malachi warned that they would be cursed with a curse if they failed to follow these divine instructions. Just what was the curse? It was a lack of rain, a lack of productivity, and a lack of success in their business. The bottom line is that *the curse was a curse of lack!*

WHAT LACKS IN YOUR LIFE?

In Hebrew, the common word for lack refers to *being deficient in something*. When someone says, "That person lacks common sense," or "He lacks wisdom," it means they are deficient in that area. From a financial perspective, continual lack will cause bills to go unpaid and eventually lead to bankruptcy or poverty. Haggi's words are parallel for our time:

> *"You have sown much, and bring in little; you eat, but do not have enough; you drink, but you are not filled with drink; you clothe yourselves, but no one is warm; and he who earns wages, earns wages to put into a bag with holes."*

The words of Haggai seem to be practical for our generation. People eat but are not satisfied, drink and are still thirsty, have clothing but are still discontent, and sow their seed and lack a harvest. Haggai said it was like throwing your money into a bag with holes. It seems people are continually falling short of goals and expectations, especially in the area of finances.

Both Haggai and Malachi understood that the first rule of defeating lack is to follow the principles of the Almighty in Scripture concerning how to create income and be a good steward over your money and possessions. When Israel refused to follow the revealed instructions of God, Haggai wrote that the people kindled a fire on the altar for nothing, offered polluted (moldy) bread on the altar, presented the lame and blind for a sacrifice, and as a result God was not receiving their offering or their rituals. This is why Malachi cried out that the people were robbing God (Mal 3:8)

We must remember that more is accomplished with the favor of God than with the favor of man. Man's favor toward you may shift with circumstances, but God's favor remains through your steadfast obedience. It is in the power of God to either command a blessing (release favor, according to Lev. 25:21) or permit a curse (release disfavor, according to Mal. 2:2).

Two examples will illustrate the enigma of this blessing and curse principle. Israel wandered forty years in the wilderness and was fed with manna falling from heaven each morning, except on the Sabbath day. The people received double on Friday, prior to the Sabbath, and the manna was preserved by God for the Sabbath day itself. If the Hebrews attempted to store it up on any of the other five days, it would develop worms or melt. Thus the blessing of provision could become a negative element if God's instructions were not properly followed (Exod. 16:15-35).

The second example is the Jubilee blessing. Every seventh day was a Sabbath of rest for the people, but every seventh year was called a Sabbatical year, in which the entire land was to rest (Lev. 25). This meant no planting, harvesting or work for the animals. The Almighty supernaturally blessed the sixth year with such increase (no lack) that the people could live from the sixth year's increase through the seventh year and even into the eighth year!

> *"Then I will command my blessing upon you in the sixth year, and it shall bring forth fruit for three years."*
>
> – LEVITICUS 25:21

Notice they would have enough fruit to enjoy for three years. This would be the sixth, seventh, and eight year—a total of three. The same occurred on every seventh cycle of seven years (49 years) in the year of the Jubilee. The challenge was that, as Israel claimed their Promised Land, they forgot to keep these seasons of rest. As a result they were eventually led into Babylonian captivity for refusing to allow the land to keep the Sabbaths.

The seventy years of captivity are explained in 2 Chronicles 36:21:

> *"To fulfill the word of the LORD by the mouth of Jeremiah, until the land had enjoyed her sabbaths: for as long as she lay desolate she kept sabbath, to fulfill threescore and ten years."*

This unusual instruction was intended to bless the people, give them rest from their work for an entire year, and bring supernatural harvest and prosperity to families owning farms. However, it actually brought the disfavor of God upon the nation for lack of obedience. If the people did not allow the land to rest, then God would force a rest by removing the people from the land. This was the theme of Malachi's warning to the people:

> *"If ye will not hear, and if ye will not lay it to heart, to give glory unto my name, says the LORD of hosts, I will even send a curse upon you, and I will curse your blessings: yea, I have cursed them already, because ye do not lay it to heart."*
>
> – MALACHI 2:2

ABRAHAM'S TENTH

Genesis 14 records that, in the time of Abraham, five foreign kings invaded the southern portion of Israel in the Dead Sea region and took captive all the people of the five cities of the plain, including Sodom. Abraham's nephew Lot and his family were also taken captive. Abraham organized 318 fighting men on camels and attacked the kings, taking back the people and the possessions of Sodom. Abraham carried the goods or spoils from the war to Jerusalem (then called Salem according to Gen. 14:18), and offered the tithe to God's priest and king, Melchizedek (Gen. 14:20). The word tithe means the tenth, thus one tenth of the spoil was given to the King-Priest of Jerusalem.

Most casual readers assume that the tithe Abraham gave was from his own wealth. However, this is not the case in this narrative. After carefully examining the text, we see that it was the goods and possessions from Sodom that Abraham used for tithe. As this event unfolded, the king of Sodom told Abraham to keep all the possessions of wealth, and just release to the king the people of the city (Gen. 14:21). But Abraham refused to take the wealth, as he desired that his blessing come from God, and for no man to receive personal glory for his financial and material blessings (Gen. 14:22-23).

Abraham was able to defeat these kings with a small group of trained servants (Gen. 14:14). Abraham was God's personal covenant man, and according to Genesis 15:1, God promised to be Abraham's shield (defender in war) and reward (financial provider).

When the five kings from the area of Shinar (near Babylon) chose to attack Sodom, they were unaware that God's covenant man, Abraham, had a nephew named Lot living in the city (Gen. 19).

When the kings captured Lot and his family, God came through to rescue Lot by sending Abraham as the deliverer. This is an example of how an *enemy of Abraham became an enemy of God*. When the kings captured Lot, God's attention went to Abraham's bloodline and God defeated the enemy.

In Genesis 18, when the outcry against Sodom and Gomorrah was great because of their wickedness, God decided to destroy them. Abraham asked Him, "Would you also destroy the righteous with the wicked?" Knowing that his nephew Lot lived in Sodom, Abraham bargained with God. Will you spare Sodom if you find fifty righteous? Forty-five? Forty, thirty, twenty? How about ten? God agreed that He would spare Sodom if he could find ten righteous in the city.

As a side note, it is interesting that Abraham tithed a tenth from the goods of Sodom, and he bargained with God to save the city if He could find as few as ten righteous.

In Genesis 19, God spared Lot by ordering his family to leave the city, although only Lot, his wife, and two daughters fled for their lives. Unfortunately, his wife died while fleeing because she looked back.

Genesis 19:29 says that *God remembered Abraham!* God gave Lot's entire family a chance to escape the destruction because of Abraham. The adversary can never defeat a person who is in covenant with God, as long as that person understands the spiritual and legal authority that is provided for them in the covenant (see Luke 10:19).

THE JERICHO CURSE

God takes seriously the promises He makes to bless and prosper His covenant people, and we in turn should take seriously the blessings and warnings He gives us in His covenant document, the Bible. The story of Achan in Joshua 6:17-19 is a prime example.

The fortified city of Jericho was surrounded by high walls and was the first of thirty-one major cities to be captured by Israel after the Israelites crossed the Jordan River and entered their Promised Land. The seizure of Jericho occurred around the time of the Feast of First Fruits, when the first of the ripened barley was to be presented to God. The law of first fruits guaranteed that, if the first of the increase of the field was presented to God, then the remaining harvest field would be blessed. Since Jericho was the *first city* to be captured and the season was first fruits, the Lord instructed that everything in the city belonged to the treasury of the Lord. This was the first fruits offering given to the Lord that would enable Israel to take the remaining thirty-one cities.

Joshua said that if anyone took possessions from Jericho for themselves, they would have an accursed thing. The Hebrew word *accursed* is used four times in Joshua 6:17-18. The Word in Hebrew is *cherem,* and refers to *shutting something in with a net where it cannot escape.* It refers to something cursed or doomed to destruction. Why would God make the spoils of Jericho accursed, yet tell the people to bring those same spoils into the treasure house of the Lord (Josh. 6:19)? First, because this was the first fruits to the Lord; and when they are given to the Lord, they are blessed. But when they are withheld, favor is restrained.

As Malachi pointed out, when we give God the tenth (tithes) He "rebukes the devourer" (Mal 3:11), but when we withhold the tenth then the curse is a curse of lack that follows. During the raid of Jericho, Achan, a man from the tribe of Judah, secretly withheld a beautiful Babylonian garment, along with gold and silver, burying them in his tent. When Achan took for himself what was intended for the House of God, not only did he suffer, but the entire army was impacted in their ability to win the next battle at Ai (see Joshua chapter 7).

Great blessings of increase and success are pronounced in Scripture upon those who willingly give of their time and finances with a cheerful attitude (2 Cor. 9:7), but lack comes to those who withhold:

> *"The generous soul will be made rich, and he who waters will also be watered himself.*
>
> *The people will curse him who withholds grain, but blessing will be on the head of him who sells it."*
>
> – PROVERBS 11:25-26 (NKJV)

WHY ARE THERE SO MANY HOLES IN YOUR BAG OF BLESSING?

Why is it difficult at times to make financial ends meet? Why are bills often overdue? Why do your finances seem to come up short? The simple answer is that personal debts are exceeding person income. You cannot have $2,500 a month in bills when you are only making $2,000 a month in income. Without payment, eventually your credit card debts will be turned over to a collector, your bank will foreclose on your home, or somebody will show up to repossess your car. Excessive spending and easy access to credit cards has wreaked havoc on individuals and families, who spend more than they take in.

Nearly one out of four Americans lives from paycheck to paycheck and has no personal savings. One out of five owes more on unsecured debt than they have in savings. The answer to this problem is to spend less, earn more and pay off debts.

One of the Bible's wealthiest men was King Solomon. He was also considered a leader with a gift of wisdom, meaning he knew how to solve problems and give solutions to complicated issues. He penned three books in the Bible: Proverbs, Song of Solomon and Ecclesiastes. In the proverbs, Solomon gave several reasons why people experience financial lack or fail in their economic and business success. These wisdom proverbs are practical for every generation.

1. EASY MONEY COMES AND EASY MONEY GOES

Solomon wrote:

> *"An inheritance may be gotten hastily at the beginning; but the end thereof shall not be blessed."*
>
> – PROV. 20:21

An inheritance is passed on to heirs through an estate that someone leaves after their death. This is usually distributed by a written will or a legal trust fund. Over the years I have heard horror stories of relatives fighting over jewelry, bank accounts, furniture, property, cars and other possessions after the death of a family member.

Do not assume that your children will know what to do with your belongings when you depart this life. If money or possessions are involved, family members will act in ways you would not have imagined. Put your desires for distribution in a legal will or trust fund, including details of each possession and to whom it is willed. When a financially unstable child (of any age), or a child with an addiction gets access to mom and dad's cash, rest assured it will be spent quickly and it will feed addictions.

My wife and I have a trust fund that says if I precede her in death, she receives all I have. Then when she dies, or if we both pass at the same time, our two children receive the inheritance. However, there is a written clause which says that, if my children are on illegal drugs, addicted to legal narcotics, or drinking any form of alcohol, they receive nothing until they can prove they are delivered and clean for a set period of time; and then the inheritance is distributed over time and not in a lump sum. As a caring father, I refuse to have what we have worked for in our earthly life used to assist either child who would not be in a spiritual condition to have the wisdom to use the inheritance wisely.

2. THE SPIRIT OF THE SLUGGARD

Often we speak of someone being lazy, or we see someone who sleeps late, or refuses to work when he has both the mind and strength to do so. In Proverbs, Solomon calls this type of person a sluggard. The Hebrew word for *sluggard* is also used by Solomon and translated as *slothful*.

There is an animal called a sloth, and there are six species of sloths that live in Central and South America. They are known for sleeping ten to eighteen hours a day, eating, and being too lazy to clean themselves. They hang upside for hours without moving. They can eat, sleep, and give birth while simply hanging from limbs of trees. They have actually been seen still hanging from a tree after their death! This is the imagery Solomon had in mind when he warned of a person being lazy and slothful. Solomon warned of the slothful and the sluggish man.

A sluggard loves sleep (Prov. 6:9), and dealing with them is an agitation, like vinegar on the teeth and smoke in the eyes (Prov. 10:26). They always desire something but are too lazy to work for it (Prov. 13:4). They will not plow because the weather is never perfect enough for them, thus they will eventually become beggars (Prov. 20:4).

A sluggard will always think he is right and everyone else is wrong (Prov. 26:16). A slothful person will always be in debt (Prov. 12:24), and will hunt food, catch it, but never cook it (Prov. 12:27). He will waste time if he is at work (Prov. 18:9) and is often too lazy to work (Prov. 21:25). A sluggard will allow weeds to grow and take no pride in his property or farm (Prov. 24:30-31).

A sloth is simply a person who is lazy and who refuses to gain knowledge, heed instruction or seek after wisdom. He will come to poverty and shame.

The world is full of sluggards who financially live off others without making an effort to support themselves with the works of their hands. Most sluggards love the concept of redistribution of wealth, which to them means that a significant share of the money someone receives from working hard should go to them for doing nothing. These Proverbs tell what happens to the sluggard and lazy person who won't accept correction:

> *"Yet a little sleep, a little slumber, a little folding of the hands to sleep: So shall thy poverty come as one that travelleth, and thy want as an armed man."*
>
>   – PROV. 6:10-11 (NKJV)

> *"Poverty and shame will come to him who disdains correction, but he who regards a rebuke will be honored."*
>
>   – PROV. 13:18

Lack will come to those who are too lazy to work for a living, or who spend their time just wasting time. The only way of breaking a lazy cycle is to enter a work cycle where your motivation is to do a job, complete it, and be rewarded for your success.

3. SIN AND HABITS OF THE FLESH

This topic was discussed briefly in another section of the book, but it is worth repeating because these things bring poverty to a person's life. Alcohol and drugs ruin lives and bring poverty, and anybody who wants to break the spirit of lack in life must give up these and other wasteful spending habits. The Bible tells us:

> *"He that loveth pleasure shall be a poor man: he that loveth wine and oil shall not be rich."*
>
> – PROV. 21:17

> *"For the drunkard and the glutton will come to poverty, and drowsiness will clothe a man with rags."*
>
> – PROVERBS 23:21

There is a reason why every major alcoholic beverage store has one big word—SPIRITS—on the advertising sign. These words are not intended to mean this, but alcohol consumption and addiction can and will open doors to demonic activity and spirits, which can only be broken when the addiction is broken.

If you live or have lived in a rural community, you know that most small towns have a "town drunk." This is the person who is never seen sober, who usually cannot keep a job, and who goes from place to place seeking a handout to purchase liquor. Thankfully, God has delivered many individuals from the grip of alcohol addiction. However, American society has made it acceptable to drink as much as you can as often as you can. One of four people has an addictive nature, and they will become addicted to something—drugs, alcohol, pornography, gambling and so forth.

In the Bible, not one good thing ever came of someone consuming alcoholic beverages. Noah got drunk, which led to his grandson Canaan being cursed (Gen. 9:25). Lot was made drunk and committed incest with his daughters (Gen. 19:34-35). Lot was so drunk that he did not even perceive when his daughters lay with him. The king of Babylon had his wild party with his leaders, during which time God's finger wrote on the wall of the palace, warning the king of an overthrow. The king and his drunken men were overthrown by the Persians and were unable to defend themselves—perhaps because they were too drunk to fight (see Dan. 5).

David made Uriah drunk in an attempt to set him up to have relations with his wife; however, Uriah refused to go home and David was punished for a series of sins he committed (see 2 Sam 11). Nabal was drunk, experienced a massive heart attack, and died a wicked man (1 Sam. 25:36-37). There is also a woe (curse) placed upon those who give strong drink to their neighbor (Hab. 2:15).

Those who spend time sipping strong drink will indeed gain "spirts," but not the type of spirits they desire. All alcoholic beverages cost money, and addiction to alcohol has cost jobs, loss of work time, and loss of license for driving under the influence of alcohol. Some people can blame their prison sentence on being drunk while driving or engaging in some other behavior that resulted in a felony conviction.

Much can also be said about the damage to the body's vital organs through alcohol abuse. I have seen anger, abuse, and poverty result because men and women come under the iron stronghold of alcohol. I have watched them go from a level of success and prosperity, to losing everything and even living on the street.

Fleshly or unclean habits are a "bag with holes in it." All habits and addictions have a financial price, as well as a physical and spiritual cost to the abuser. Below is an example of the cost of various habits. I have included three of the most common so-called pleasure habits that people engage in—smoking cigarettes, drinking beer, and smoking marijuana. These costs are only estimated as prices change and vary by region and so on:

The Habit	Cost per Item
Cigarettes	$5 or more a pack
Six Pack of beer	$6
Pot	$40 for 1/8 oz.

Depending on a person's usage, you can see how costs can add up quickly. If the person is addicted to street drugs, such as crack or meth, the costs are even higher. At times I think people never sit down and consider how much they spend on habits each month. Then when they can't make their monthly obligations, when utility bills go unpaid and groceries cannot be purchased, they wonder where their money went.

This is why drug addicts are often thieves. The crimes they commit to get money to buy drugs will oftentimes land them in prison. Great job opportunities are rare for those who have served time in prison for a felony conviction.

A person who persists in these habits should be certain to have good hospital and life insurance, as later in life it is quite possible they may get certain forms of cancer, cirrhosis of the liver, emphysema, or a loss of brain activity. Smoking just one cigarette can take several minutes off your life.

A police and former drug enforcement officer in my home town said that there are eight million people in America addicted to methamphetamines, and only six percent fully recover from their addiction. Ninety six percent of those who turn to Christ, receive the redemptive covenant, and follow the Scriptures recover from the addiction. My heart breaks when I see someone addicted to drugs.

Addictions will bring lack, suffering, and poverty to the abuser. There are many good places in the nation that deal with addictions, and people are willing to help anybody who is willing to become whole, healed, and delivered through prayer, counseling, building new friendships and relationships, and the power of the Holy Spirit.

4. THE ADDICTION OF GAMBLING

Many Americans are addicted to gambling, called by the professional name of "the gaming industry." When I fill up my vehicle with gasoline, I often see people handing out five, ten, or twenty dollars and more to purchase a roll of cards, hoping to scratch off a big hit. One store manager told me about a man who spent $300 for cards and won fifty dollars. The fellow was jumping for joy. He was excited that he gave away $250 to win $50.

If you told these people that you'd like to make a deal with them—give me a hundred dollars and I will give you back twenty—they would laugh and say, "You think I'm crazy?" Yet they turn over this kind of money for gambling because they believe that one day they will beat the odds.

Here are some statistics about Americans and gambling:

- 85% of the people in America have placed a bet at least once

- 2.5 million Americans have a gambling addiction

- Casinos make $30 Billion and lotteries make $17 billion a year

- Those making under $10,000 play lotto three times more often than those making $50,000, although gambling in general occurs more often in high income households (72%) versus lower income households (55%)

- Teens: 42% of 14-year-olds, 63% of 16-year-olds, and 76% of 18-year-olds gamble

- When Atlantic City set up gambling, the crime within a 30-mile radius increased by 100%

- Americans have spent $500 billion on wagers (bets)

- Families who have a family member with a gambling addiction have higher rates of domestic violence and child abuse

You have a better chance of being struck by lightning on a clear day, and at the same time be hit by a car and having a heart attack, than you do of winning the big lottery. Yet it is the few stories of unexpected wins and overnight millionaires that hook multitudes into spending needed money to get that winning number. Recently, one man withdrew $30,000 of his life savings to purchase tickets, just to increase his chance of winning America's biggest lottery. He won nothing.

Gambling is the proverbial "thrill of the chase." Once a person does occasionally win at a slot machine, black jack table or some other form of gambling, the addiction is set and the mind tells them that if they spend more, they will win more. The fact is, machines at the casino are set against your favor and not for your benefit. Often they state huge amounts of money they have paid out, without telling you the massive numbers of people who took chances and spent hundreds of millions of dollars in the process.

Compulsive gambling is an addiction that feeds the same pleasure areas of the brain that are fed with pornography, drug addiction and such. Dopamine is released in the brain at the possibility of winning. Some suggest that lower levels of serotonin in the brain can cause a person to be at higher risk for pathological gambling. If you continually think about gambling, seek out money to gamble, and cannot resist buying scratch-off cards when in a convenience store, then you have the symptoms of addiction.

Dangerous debts will be incurred by gambling, and much money will be wasted that could have been invested for retirement. Imagine the reward a person could store up for eternity had they spent some of that money for the work of the Kingdom of God. Instead, the money was thrown into a bottomless pit, just to take a chance on winning that which a person cannot resist in order to please the flesh.

Freedom from these addictions requires rewiring of the thought process of the brain and a change of bad patterns of habit. A person needs spiritual help, psychological help, and the power of the Holy Spirit to overcome serious addictions.

5. SCAMS AND COUNTERFEITS

Counterfeits have always been a lucrative way for unscrupulous individuals to make money from innocent victims. Look at how money has been counterfeited over the years. People have even counterfeited pennies. For example, there is a penny in which only twelve were made.

It was a steel penny that was accidently minted with copper, and they are rare and valuable. It is astonishing that someone would counterfeit a penny, hoping it would sell for thousands of dollars. There is also a rare, three-legged buffalo nickel, minted in the 1930's. Counterfeiters learned to take an ordinary buffalo nickel and file off the a leg to pass it off as a genuine three legged buffalo, thus making money. Only an expert can see the difference. I have collected sports cards for years, and sometimes the most expensive cards sold on the Internet are counterfeit. Old oil paintings that look authentic can actually be reproductions.

Then there are scams. A scam is a fraudulent business scheme designed to make a quick profit. Scams hit 30.2 million adults in the United States, and many of them originate in other countries. This problem is perhaps the saddest for Christians, as many good, honest believers have been invited to participate in a new form of investment that is guaranteed to make them millionaires. Those offering the opportunity often use embellished stories or testimonials from those participating in the plan, in order to gain the trust of others to reel them in. Often Scriptures are quoted, "The wealth of the wicked is laid up for the just," to confirm from the Bible that certainly this investment is the one that God Himself predicted!

Christians become easy targets for what is called "affinity fraud," as investment scams prey upon religious groups and communities, including ethnic groups. The first strategy is to enlist known religious leaders, sometimes giving them a monetary benefit to prove the investment works. Religious leaders were then unknowingly used by scammers to encourage congregational members to invest. Many of the past and possibly present day scams are called Ponzi or pyramid schemes.

Any investment should be checked out in great detail, and not just by listening to the words of others. One of the clearest signs of a scam is when a promise is made of a huge financial return for a minimal investment. The facts are, if an investment seems too good to be true, then history shows that it usually isn't true. One man promised that with your $1,000 investment, you will eventually receive up to $100,000! He offers currency and has been claiming for years that any day now the big return is coming. If this were true, then why isn't his company holding on to the very thing they are offering instead of selling it to others, if they will receive such a huge return?

If some of these investments were so lucrative, then there should be massive numbers of solid businessmen swallowing up the investments. Instead, government websites warn of scams, but so many choose to believe in the words of the one doing the promising, and it is impossible to convince them otherwise.

The second thing a scammer wants is your banking information and social security number. For many years, people and even churches have received e-mails stating that a rich Christian died and has left millions of dollars in a European or African bank for them. All they need is your banking information and $2,000 to release this wealth from a European or African bank, and you will suddenly be rich.

I have read the e-mails and have had people call our office telling us they just received this and are planning on supporting the ministry with it. Their intention is so pure, yet some have wired money only to realize later it was all a fabrication. Millions of dollars have been lost and personal savings accounts wiped out with these scams. Even certain African banks and their presidents were part of the scams, providing false information to the person and in return taking their account numbers and draining their personal bank account in the U.S. dry. Hundreds of these scams originated in Nigeria after the income from oil declined many years ago. Here is an example of one letter that was sent:

> "I have been requested by the Nigerian National Petroleum Company to contact you for assistance in resolving a matter. The Nigerian National Petroleum Company has recently concluded a large number of contracts of oil exploration in the sub-Sahara region. The contracts have immediately produced monies equaling US $40,000,000. The Nigerian National Petroleum Company is desirous of oil explorations in other parts of the world. However, because of certain regulations of the Nigerian Government, it is unable to move these funds to another region.

"Your assistance is requested as a non-Nigerian citizen to assist the Nigerian National Petroleum Company and also the Central Bank of Nigeria, in moving these funds out of Nigeria. If the funds can be transferred to your name, in your United States account, then you can forward the funds as directed by the Nigerian National Petroleum Company. They would agree to allow you to retain 10% or US $4 million of this amount.

"However, to be a legitimate transferee of these moneys according to Nigerian law, you must presently be a depositor of at least US $100,000 in a Nigerian bank which is regulated by the central bank of Nigeria. If it will be possible for you to assist us, we would be most grateful. We suggest that you meet with us in person in Lagos, and that during your visit I will introduce you to the representatives of the Nigerian National Petroleum Company as well as certain officials of the central bank of Nigeria.

"Please call me at your earliest convenience at (phone number inserted) time is of essence in this matter, very quickly the Nigerian government will realize the Central Bank is maintaining this amount on deposit and attempt to levy certain depository taxes on it."

YOURS TRULY BEN AHORE

This type of letter was sent as a scam to get a person's banking information and transfer money from the person's account without their knowledge. And since the scam originates in another country, there is nothing the person can do to have their money returned or see the scammer brought to justice. So the scams continue, and gullible people lose hundreds of thousands of dollars.

If someone e-mails you, text messages you, or calls on your phone posing as your bank, insurance company, the IRS, or anybody else requesting your banking numbers or social security numbers, never give them out! Your bank, insurance company, and the IRS have that information already. Never confirm numbers over the phone to someone you do not personally know, as this is another method of gaining access to your information.

These scams work because they feed off two desires: one carnal and one spiritual. The carnal is our greed—to get rich quick, to have it made, to never have to work hard again and to do whatever we want. The second is a true desire to help spread the gospel and reach souls. This is the saddest part of a religious scam, when sincere people who desire to bless the kingdom are taken advantage of and suffer because of the deception of a scam artist. Christians are an easy target because they believe the best in people, and they are too trusting to spot a liar and a fraud.

With computer fraud, hackers and modern technology, each believer must be made aware of the scams and learn to be discerning. If you can invest a little and bring in one hundred to one thousand times more in return, then history proves that someone has invented a good gimmick to get your money.

6. GET OUT OF DEBT

Moving from debt increase to debt reduction works wonders to close the hole in your wallet. There are numerous specialists in this field who offer books, audio CDs and DVDs, or classes that offer techniques to help reduce your debt and bring spending under control. Start now to work toward becoming debt free. Learn how to properly handle money.

In the late 1990s, David Wilkerson wrote a book in which he encouraged people to become debt free because a severe economic crisis was coming in the future. People mocked him at the time, because the economy and the stock market were booming. Nobody could foresee an economic crisis or depression anywhere in America's future. David was even called a false prophet by some self-proclaimed heresy hunters.

But now we are experiencing the times of which he spoke. In retrospect, we can see that the Lord was giving His people an opportunity to use the following decade to get out of debt. Instead of spending unnecessarily and purchasing larger and more expensive items, that money could have wisely been used to pay off mortgages and save for the future.

Years ago, Wilkerson also saw a time when the government would be in such terrible financial condition that they would be unable to pay people who are receiving forms of government assistance. He also saw the day when there would be a strong public backlash against unions—particularly public service employee unions. When Americans are suffering economically, they don't want more money taken from their limited income to keep public service employees and union leaders financially well off.

Today we are on the verge of the fulfillment of both of these events. We have already seen what happened to Greece as a result of the demands of their public service unions and unionized employees. Greed and dishonesty bring trouble upon both the household and the nation (Prov. 15:27).

7. SPEND ON NEEDS AND NOT WANTS

This is a simple truth, mentioned earlier in the book. Why spend large sums of money on things that are not actually needs and will not benefit you spiritually, emotionally, physically, or in some other form. You will never lose when investing in the three principle things Solomon wrote about—knowledge, understanding and wisdom.

8. SPEND ON THAT WHICH BRINGS A RETURN

In the following verses, God is telling His people to move away from spending on those things that do not truly satisfy, and instead, place their faith, trust and desires in Him in order to satisfy the soul:

> *"Ho, every one that thirsteth, come ye to the waters, and he that hath no money; come ye, buy, and eat; yea, come, buy wine and milk without money and without price.*

> *"Wherefore do ye spend money for that which is not bread? and your labour for that which satisfieth not? hearken diligently unto me, and eat ye that which is good, and let your soul delight itself in fatness."*
>
> – ISAIAH 55:1-2

One of the outstanding promises in the Scripture for those who have been obedient to the Lord is found in Hebrews 10:35-36:

> *"Cast not away therefore your confidence, which hath great recompense of reward.*

"For ye have need of patience, that, after ye have done the will of God, ye might receive the promise."

Another translation renders this verse as:

"Do not, therefore, fling away your fearless confidence, for it carries a great and glorious compensation of reward.

"For you have need of steadfast patience and endurance, so that you may perform and fully accomplish the will of God, and thus receive and carry away [and enjoy to the full] what is promised."

– HEBREWS 10:35-36 (AMP)

There is a special "recompense of reward" when believers follow the instructions of the New Covenant. In the Greek, the word recompense is *misthapodosia,* and it can allude to a reimbursement or compensation of some form. The idea is that you are sent out on an assignment for work, and in the process you need food, transportation, a place to rest, and other needs. You keep a receipt for all expenditures and, upon returning, you turn in the receipts and the company reimburses you for your expenses.

Our rewards for obedience might not come immediately after we have enacted the will of God. This is why it requires both patience to endure and confidence that it will come to pass. Your confidence in God as the unshakable rock and your patience will give you the ability to endure long seasons without seeing results.

When you enter into a redemptive covenant through Christ, you not only receive eternal life, but you also open a door for change that positively alters your emotional, spiritual and economic situation. Part of the covenant of blessing for a believer is prosperity in the true sense, where you are in health and able to enjoy life without habitual distractions and hindrances. Breaking free from addictions will bring relief to your mind and spirit. By breaking habits, you will save your money and health, and extend your days on earth.

Once you have received Christ, then begin to study the principles in proverbs, the wisdom of the men of the Bible, and the words of Jesus that deal with personal issues of life, including how to live a disciplined and righteous life, how to maintain faith, how to witness to others, how to give of your time and finances to the Kingdom work and so on. By learning and practicing these principles, you will increase your knowledge and become a valuable asset in your place of employment and your church. This takes discipline and motivation, but you will not regret the end results.

You can sew up the bag with holes in it by giving to the work of the Lord to advance His Kingdom. You can learn to spend wisely and invest only in things that have spiritual, physical or family value. For example, I see a family vacation, not as a waste of money, but as a valuable time to relax, make memories, and spend time with my family away from ministry cares and earthly distractions. I also view attending Word-centered conferences an investment in the person's spiritual welfare, and they also help you meet and fellowship with other believers who can encourage you and pray for your needs. Attending a local church and weekly services is an investment in your future, and spending time in prayer is a great benefit. Giving is a true source of blessing, with both an earthly and a heavenly return!

OBEDIENCE, TRUST AND WISDOM

We must remember that the spiritual blessings promised in the New Covenant do not operate simply because they are inspired and printed in a Bible. The Word of God works when you take the instructions, follow them, speak them, and act upon them. When our problems are linked with recession, economic shaking and job changes, we must remember that the covenant of blessing does not hinge on the circumstances as we see them. Your faith in God can take you to places you have never been, allow you to meet people you have never before met, work a job you never thought you could have, and receive resources that are an unexpected blessing.

In these last days, the greatest blessings will come to those who put their trust in the Lord rather than man, the government, or handouts. Those who have passed the tests and proven they can be trusted to use the financial blessings to advance the Kingdom of God will be given the resources to do so.

God will reward the people who are already proven givers. He will reward those who can properly discern the times and listen to the voice of the Holy Spirit. These people will have unique insight into what God is doing on earth and will know where the money should be spent. They will pay attention to the Lord's direction and have wisdom to properly use the money for the advancement of the end-time Kingdom of God.

Let me also add that the nation that commits idolatry, sheds innocent blood, legalizes abominations, and turns its back on Israel will not be blessed because it has brought upon itself a curse. But God's people are a nation unto God—a nation within a nation. God will supernaturally provide for His obedient and righteous people by using the methods mentioned in this book, and perhaps even others.

Use the gifts God gave you to earn a living, and when He blesses the works of your hands, use the money wisely. Remember that you will never take any earthly belonging with you into the next life. But you will take the people who were won to Christ through the seeds you sowed into the Kingdom of God. You can either lay up your treasures here on earth, where you have use of them until you die, or you can store your treasures in heaven, where you will have use of them for eternity!

> *"Lay not up for yourselves treasures upon earth, where moth and rust doth corrupt, and where thieves break through and steal; But lay up for yourselves treasures in heaven, where neither moth nor rust doth corrupt, and where thieves do not break through nor steal; For where your treasure is, there will your heart be also."*
>
> – MATTHEW 6:19-21